COACHING THE DEFENSIVE BACKFIELD

Greg McMackin

Harding Press
Haworth, New Jersey 07641

Copyright © 1992 *by*

Harding Press

Library of Congress Cataloging-in-Publication Data

McMackin, Greg.
   Coaching the defensive backfield / Greg McMackin.
     p.   cm.
   ISBN 0-9624779-3-1
   1. Football—Defense. 2. Backfield play (Football) 3. Football-
-Coaching. I. Title.
   GV951.18.M42   1992
   796.332′2—dc20   91-43957
                                           CIP

Printed in the United States of America

ISBN 0-9624779-3-1

HARDING PRESS
P.O. Box 141
Haworth, NJ 07641
Books by and for the coaching profession

Contents

Acknowledgments

Thank you to my wife, Heather, and daughter, Shannon, for their love, loyalty and friendship. Without them this book would never have been written.

Thanks, also, to Frank and Elise McMackin for all their years of love and support.

Introduction

Coaching the Defensive Backfield is a complete text on the coaching of all facets of defensive secondary play through the teaching and coaching of exacting fundamentals, game-like drills and effective game-day strategies. Theories and designs of coverages are thoroughly examined by analyzing such subjects as zones of the field, formation, motion, backfield set recognition and pass pattern coverage.

A comprehensive analysis of secondary play is explored through the examination of selected basic man-to-man, zone and blitz coverages and their fundamental techniques. In addition, you are presented with coordinated game-like teaching drills and in-depth coaching points that will enable your secondary to precisely execute such important concepts as bump and run, shuffle, jam, blitz, hash, leverage and run support techniques.

The defensive back must be one of the most effective and thoroughly coached players on your football team. He is constantly put in crucial game-deciding situations where he must often defend the fastest and most skilled players on the opposing team. One false step, stumble or missed assignment by a secondary defender can result in a devastatingly long gain or possible game-losing touchdown. By learning such important ideas as proper positioning, corner and safety support, defending the streak route and collisioning the post route, your defensive backs will be able to consistently come up with those big plays which so often mean the difference between victory and defeat.

Coaching the Defensive Backfield will help you to teach and coach your secondary to produce team-motivating interceptions, fumbles and fumble recoveries.

Your defensive backs must be thoroughly prepared in all phases of secondary play if your total defensive effort is to be effective. This book will help make your players proficient in such skills as footwork, playing the ball and tackling. It will help your players to develop a knowledge of secondary play that will lead to the precise execution of assignments that produce those drive-stopping turnovers.

Coaching the Defensive Backfield is a thorough study of all the fundamentals, techniques and drills you will need to produce a successful secondary year in and year out. You are presented with such secondary theories of coverage as zone, man-to-man and blitz. You are then shown the specific techniques and drills you will need to produce game-winning execution. You will be shown how to effectively utilize such secondary designs as Three-Deep Zone, Two-Deep Zone, Man and Man Free, Two-Deep Man and Blitz to shut down any run, pass or multiple offense attacks.

Coaching the Defensive Backfield allows you to prepare your secondary defenders through a complete plan concerning skills, techniques and game-like drills that will help you to produce a fundamentally sound, aggressive and exciting defensive backfield. Interception techniques, tackling, keys and reads, stripping the ball, defending man and zone pass routes, stuffing the run, zone techniques, man techniques, position on a receiver, proper footwork and game-like drills are just a few of the topics that are clearly presented to help you produce a defensive backfield that is the strength of your defense.

1

Characteristics of a Successful Defensive Back

There are many qualities that are necessary in the makeup of a successful defensive back. While coaches may have different ideas as to the most important characteristic of a defensive back, most will agree that the qualities of quickness, speed, balance, intelligence, attitude, intensity and size are necessary to allow an athlete to excel.

PLAYER CHARACTERISTICS

Quickness

When selecting the characteristics of a successful defensive back, one of the most important qualities to be considered is the athlete's quickness. The coordinated ability of a person to move his feet, hands, arms and body rapidly is even more important than speed in pass defense. A good athlete can execute a quick or accelerated burst which allows him to make the big play. He can also flick away the ball with his hands before the receiver puts the ball away.

Reaction and quickness go hand in hand. The ability to react involves quickness and refers to an individual's instant action to any movement of an opponent or to movement of the ball. The defensive back's ability to react from both a physical and mental standpoint will determine success or failure in pass defense. Reaction to a key, ball, receiver, ball carrier or block must be instantaneous.

Speed

Speed is, of course, an important part of the player's makeup. He will be covering the fastest opposing players on the field and, therefore, must be able to run. Technique, playing the ball and football knowledge will aid the athlete's play if his speed is lacking.

The defensive back must be aware of the help that is available to him from his teammates and needs to know where they are in relation to his position on the field in order to take the advantage and make the play.

Balance

A good defensive back needs the ability to maintain his balance in the execution of various football fundamentals, regardless of his body movement or direction by an opponent, even if temporary body control is lost. The ability of a player to regain his equilibrium after a slip or false step will often be the determining factor in success or failure.

Aggressiveness

Aggressiveness is another important characteristic of a good defensive back. His willingness to hit a ball carrier, receiver, or blocker, or go after the ball on a fumble or pass with the utmost degree of intensity should be one of his best assets and best weapons. An aggressive defensive back makes things happen. He breaks up passes, neutralizes receivers and blockers, causes fumbles and fumble recoveries, generates great team momentum and wins games.

Intelligence

Intelligence is, without question, an important quality in a defensive back. With the complexity of the game of football he must be able to acquire and retain knowledge. He must perform assignments correctly and effectively under game conditions, and he must make week to week or play to play adjustments according to formation tendencies, motion and audibles.

Attitude

The one ingredient that encompasses every phase of football and every phase of life is attitude. It entails the player's outlook and viewpoint regarding all phases of football and the numerous personal relationships that he encounters every day. A player with a good attitude believes that his team is going to win. Championships are won because maximum effort must come from within each and every individual reacting to every play as one unit. A player with a good attitude will also work on the weakest phase of his ability, keeping his strong points sharp.

Intensity

The quality of intensity is exhibited by the player who performs with the ultimate degree of thought, energy and force, and does so with the greatest amount of emotion. An intense player is eager, persistent and relentless in his play. He is easily motivated and has a high degree of concentration. He usually has a burning desire to compete and to succeed.

Size

Size is a factor, but it is many times overemphasized. It is more important to have an athlete who has a high lean body weight composition with a low body fat content. The main factor is to find the lean muscular weight that enables a player to maintain his strength, power, quickness and speed.

SECONDARY POSITION CHARACTERISTICS

All good secondaries take on a certain characteristic, or personality. A coach does not necessarily know what personality his defensive backfield will possess, but he should be aware of the requirements for each position.

Corner Characteristics

A corner must be your best one-on-one pass defender. He has to be one of the best athletes on the team because he will be defending the fastest players in one-on-one situations whether the coverage is man or zone. He must be fast and athletic enough to play the pass, but must also be tough and physical enough to support the opponent's running game. The corner's concentration must be complete because one lapse by his mind or body could result in a touchdown. The corner has to have great confidence. He cannot be afraid of getting beat. If he does get beat, he has to react in a positive way and make the play the next time he is tested. The corner is the thoroughbred of the secondary.

Free Safety Characteristics

The free safety should be the spark plug of the pass defense. He should be the leader in encouraging his teammates to communicate or "talk." He should call out down and distance so the other deep backs can hear him. The free safety should be a center fielder and go to the football. He should see the ball leave the passer's hand. This will enable him to get more interceptions and increase the distance he can cover. He should be intelligent and study the actions of the passer to know exactly where he will throw. He should watch the passer's eyes to take him to the ball. He must possess confidence, and when the ball is in the air, believe that it belongs to him. The free safety must be physical enough to make open-field tackles. He must be consistent, because many times he has the last chance to make the "game-saving" tackle on his opponent.

Strong Safety Characteristics

The strong safety has the same characteristics that we have previously discussed; however, he has to be more physical both in stature and in play. In many defenses he will be the primary force man. When it is a passing play he will be asked to defend the tight end, who is usually a bigger, more physical player than a wide receiver. The strong safety also has to be intelligent to call strengths and any audibles which may occur during the course of the game.

2

Basic Fundamental Techniques and Drills for Coaching the Defensive Backfield

A defensive back has to be competent in certain fundamentals that pertain to his position and most coverages. He must be able to execute at a high degree of consistency such basic techniques as stance, footwork, playing the ball, tackling and his positioning on his opponent. The fundamentals discussed in this chapter may not be specific to a particular coverage, but they are universal to obtaining excellence as a defensive back.

STANCE

A proper stance will help the defensive back be physically and mentally alert. He should never be careless in taking his stance but should always work for "cat-like" movement. Many times a flaw in footwork technique can be directly attributed to the defensive back's stance.

The proper body position should start with the knees bent and the hips lowered. This crouch is important to the player because it prevents him from coming out of his stance too high on his takeoff. The weight should be forward on his front foot and distributed on the balls of his feet. It is important that his takeoff always be from his forward foot. His shoulders should be forward with his hands hanging loosely by his side.

The defensive back's eyes should be focused on his coverage key, be it a specific receiver or the quarterback. He should be alert and relaxed.

Players will vary in stance, but they must consistently be in proper body position to get a smooth, low takeoff in their backpedal.

FOOTWORK

One of the most important fundamentals in a defensive back's makeup is his footwork. Proper footwork enables an athlete to keep the proper lateral and vertical position on his opponent. Good footwork also allows the defensive back the ability to eliminate the false step backward when breaking on a ball that is thrown in front of him. He must also have good footwork technique to execute his turns to break on balls that are thrown deeper. He should avoid crossing his feet or taking extra steps, as the result of poor footwork.

When executing proper backpedal technique, the athlete should push off his front foot and keep his feet close to the ground, no wider than six inches apart. He should feel he is running backwards the same way he runs forward. His cleats should feel as though they are slightly brushing the grass on each stride. The step, or stride, should not be too long. He should be relaxed and take comfortable strides. He should use his arms running backwards just like he does when he runs forward. It is important to keep the toes pointed straight ahead and the weight always evenly distributed over the balls of the feet. The forward lean must be maintained from the stance throughout the backpedal.

When the defensive back breaks out of his backpedal, the back foot should be planted at a 45-degree angle. This technique allows for the largest surface of the foot to come in contact with the turf. He should get as many cleats into the grass as possible. This will eliminate the false drop step. The front foot contacts the ground quickly after the plant, which allows good explosion toward the interception point. The plant position should resemble a sprinter coming out of the blocks in track.

FOOTWORK DRILLS

Drill #1: Backpedal

Purpose: In order to be a good defender, one must learn to run backwards. This drill aids in teaching the proper backpedal technique.

Procedure: From a good football stance, have four or more athletes push off their front feet and begin backpedalling for 10 yards. The players' stance and backpedal can be observed and taught. To teach and demonstrate to each individual player, the drill can be slowed down by observing one player at a time. (See Diagram 2-1.)

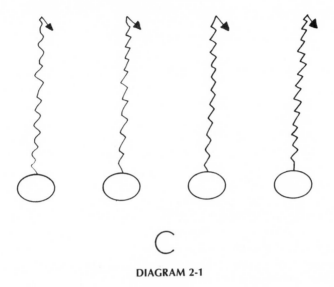

DIAGRAM 2-1

Coaching Points: When being taught, the drill should be performed with the defensive backs backpedalling on yard lines, five yards apart. The drill should be taught at a slow pace to enhance the emphasis of learning the backpedal technique.

Drill #2: Backpedal and Break

Purpose: This drill combines the break, or stopping of the backpedal, with the backpedal. The same procedure is utilized in this drill as in the Backpedal Drill.

Procedure: The coach will signal when the player breaks. The defender should break front, right, left and back. (See Diagram 2-2.)

Coaching Points: To overemphasize the forward lean, the player should touch the ground to get himself in the proper body lean position. When using a ball in drills, the defensive back should not be taught to touch the ground because he needs to concentrate on the ball.

Drill #3: M-Drill

Purpose: To teach a defensive back to break toward the line of scrimmage from a backpedal.

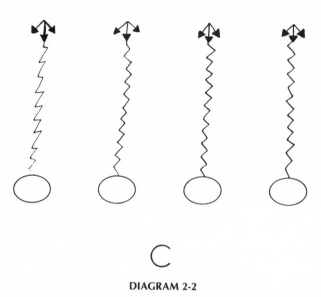

C

DIAGRAM 2-2

Procedure: The players form a single line on the sideline standing on a yard-line stripe. The first man in line begins the drill by backpedalling to the next five-yard stripe and then planting the foot away from the direction he is going to break at a 45-degree angle back toward the original line. One can repeat the procedure at intervals of 10 yards and 15 yards. (See Diagram 2-3.)

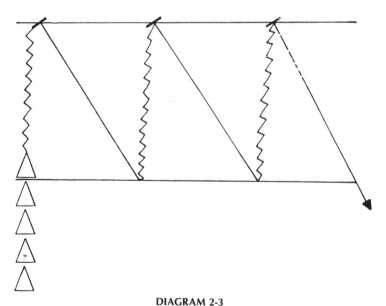

DIAGRAM 2-3

Coaching Points: The players should stay low in their backpedal, with their feet no wider apart than six inches. They must stay in a good forward lean and have good body balance. To overemphasize the forward lean, the athletes can be coached to touch the ground with their front hand at the break.

Drill #4: Backpedalling and Shuffle

Purpose: To teach the proper shuffle after backpedalling. The same organizational procedure is used as when performing the M-Drill. This drill can also be called M-Drill with a Shuffle.

Procedure: From the backpedal the defensive back will go into a shuffle for two or three steps, which enables him to get his knees turned as he prepares to turn and run with an opponent. (See Diagram 2-4.)

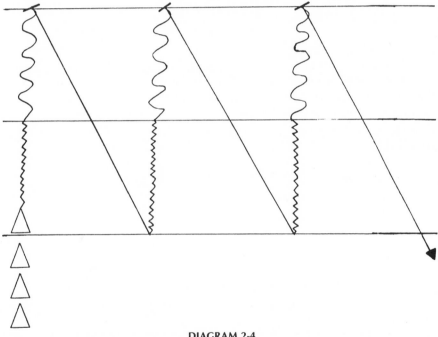

DIAGRAM 2-4

Coaching Points: The player turns both feet at a 45-degree angle to the inside and into a shuffle, or slide step. This technique is used when the defensive back has good position on his opponent and is waiting to read his move. It is important that the feet do not move past a 45-degree angle so that the defensive back can break in any direction, and also be capable of running deep with a receiver.

When executing the shuffle it is important to stay low, therefore aiding elimination of the false step. To maintain proper weight forward, the front hand should be in front of the knee and the armpit should be over the kneecap.

Drill #5: Backpedal, Shuffle and Break Drill (B.S.B.)

Purpose: To combine all of the defensive back's footwork technique. The drill is performed in the same manner as the Backpedal Drill, only now it includes the shuffle and break on the coach's signal.

Procedure: The defender should break front, right, left and back. (See Diagram 2-5.)

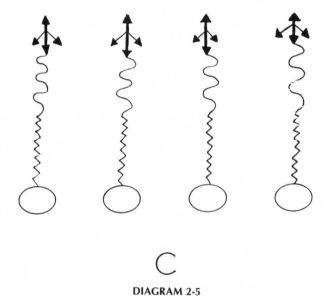

C

DIAGRAM 2-5

Coaching Points: The signal for the shuffle should be given after the defensive back has backpedalled five to ten yards. The break signal should be given by the coach with a ball indicating right, left, front or back. The coaching points utilized in teaching the backpedal, shuffle and break should be combined when using the Backpedal, Shuffle and Break Drill.

Drill #6: React to Me Drill

Purpose: To teach a defender to react to a coach's command while he is performing various defensive back footwork techniques and movements.

Procedure: The drill is performed with the players beginning by going away from the coach. The player lines up five yards away from the coach, facing him. As the coach raises the ball, the defender backpedals, then shuffles. At any time during the drill the coach can imitate any action to force the defender to react. If the coach imitates the action of handing the ball off, the defender would break to make the tackle. If the coach turns his shoulder to the right, the player would break at a 90-degree angle in that direction. The coach can either throw the ball or imitate another action, such as drop back further, which means the defender must turn and run deep. Any combination of actions can be done. (See Diagram 2-6.)

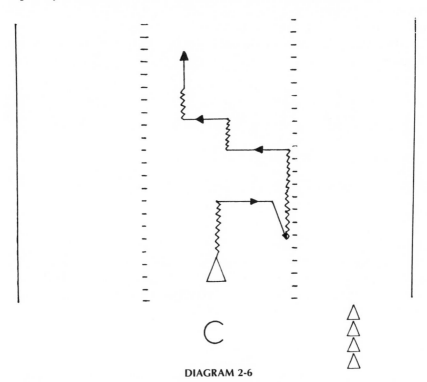

DIAGRAM 2-6

Coaching Points: Recognition, reaction, need for keeping the eyes on the ball or quarterback and breaking on the ball are all techniques that should be emphasized when using this drill. All-out effort should also be stressed as this is a good conditioning drill.

Drill #7: Wave Drill

Purpose: To teach the player body balance, quickness and coordination while changing direction at a 180-degree angle.

Procedure: To begin the drill, have three men five yards apart facing the coach. On command, the coach gives a direction with a ball, waving the players either right or left. The players push off their outside leg and step with their inside leg in the direction the coach has given. The defensive backs keep their eyes on the coach and sprint full speed in the initial direction until the coach changes their direction. They then plant their outside foot and pivot on the ball of that foot and step in the opposite direction with their inside foot and repeat the initial movement. To end the drill, the coach points the ball toward the ground and the defensive backs plant their outside foot making a 90-degree turn, and then sprint past the coach. (See Diagram 2-7.)

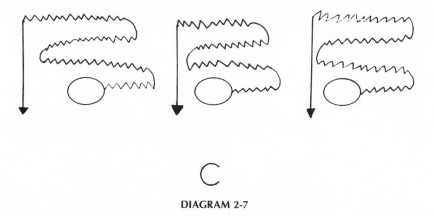

DIAGRAM 2-7

Coaching Points: It is important for the defensive back to stay low when he plants his outside foot to make his change of direction. This drill can be used as a conditioning drill and is excellent for teaching the defender balance and quickness when changing direction.

Drill #8: Running the Line

Purpose: To develop quickness, body balance and agility while changing direction running backwards.

Procedure: To begin the drill, have one man on a line facing the coach. On the coach's command, the defensive back backpedals full speed and then rotates his hips right or left. To end the drill, the coach throws the ball and the player plants his foot and breaks to the ball, then sprints past the coach. (See Diagram 2-8.)

Coaching Points: The player should keep a low plane when changing direction. The defensive back should lift the inside knee high and slip it around quickly for balance. He should use his arms when turning, keeping them close to his body and powerfully whipping the inside elbow for speed in turning the trunk of the body. The participants in the drill should sprint as hard as they can, always maintaining a low center of gravity.

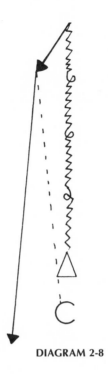

DIAGRAM 2-8

Drill #9: Backpedal Carioca

Purpose: To develop footwork and hip-girdle flexibility.

Procedure: The drill begins with three or four defenders aligning on different yard lines, and on the movement of the ball the players commence backpedalling. After three to five yards of backpedalling, the coach indicates a direction and the defenders begin the Carioca technique. When the coach gives a second signal, the defensive backs turn and go. (See Diagram 2-9.)

Coaching Points: The coach should indicate the direction that the Carioca will be executed before the drill begins. The defensive back should keep a low level of body plane with his head and shoulders down and his chin forward. The arms should swing naturally. Both short and long strides should be utilized in this drill. Perform the Carioca in both directions. When the athlete finishes, he should turn and go.

Drill #10: Speed Backpedal

Purpose: To teach the defensive back to reach with the rear foot and to increase speed. Horizontal and vertical cushion on a receiver is also taught.

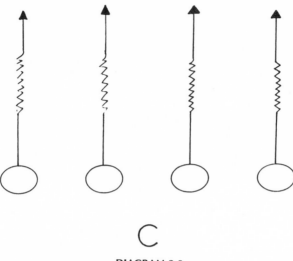

DIAGRAM 2-9

Procedure: The defenders work in pairs on lines. One to four pairs work at the same time. The defender lines up six to seven yards from the receiver on either the outside or the inside shoulder. On the command of the coach the receiver sprints as fast as he can. The defender must backpedal and maintain proper cushion as long as he can. At 10 to 15 yards the receiver will plant and run a stop or continue running. The defender must turn and run when his cushion has been broken. (See Diagram 2-10.)

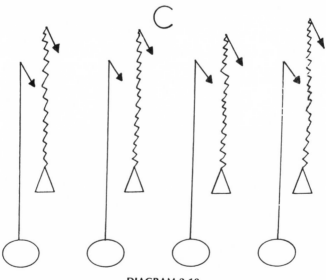

DIAGRAM 2-10

Coaching Points: The coach stands behind the defenders to help them with the proper cushion and to tell them when to turn. The defensive backs must maintain proper inside or outside alignment. The players must stay on the lines throughout the drill. If the receiver runs a stop the defender should break to the receiver.

Drill #11: Backpedal Crossover Recover

Purpose: The defensive back learns to come out of his backpedal into a crossover when the receiver has reduced the vertical cushion and to come out of his crossover into the proper recover technique, which enables him to close on the ball.

Procedure: The defensive back faces the coach and begins to backpedal on the movement of the coach, who simulates a quarterback. The coach will signal to come out of the backpedal into the crossover, and a second signal will indicate the recover technique. (See Diagram 2-11.)

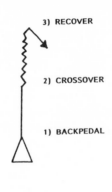

3) RECOVER

2) CROSSOVER

1) BACKPEDAL

DIAGRAM 2-11

Coaching Points: Emphasis should be given to the location of the chin and shoulders and to the arm and hand movement. Movement should stay low on the recovery technique. When turning, the player should drive the elbow to the opposite hip and snap the head. The defender should drive his brake foot into the ground and burst to the reception area. He must not round off the angle to the reception area.

PROPER POSITION ON A RECEIVER

A defensive back's position on a receiver both laterally and vertically is a key point that one must execute to be successful and is illustrated in Diagram 2-12. The proper position is derived from where the defensive back is on the field, down and distance, coverage called and where his help is. The player should remember that the position he has on a receiver is highly important in pass defense. The most difficult position to maintain is the vertical position. More defenders are beaten because of improper vertical position than any other factor. Knowledge of the receiver's release will be the greatest aid in holding and maintaining this position.

The vertical position, or distance between the receiver and the defensive back, should start at alignment. One common error when maintaining proper cushion is lining up too close to the receiver. The receiver's speed must be taken into consideration when deciding upon the proper alignment cushion.

The defensive back must push off his front foot and get into his backpedal at the precise moment the receiver takes his first step. If the defender does not get a good takeoff, his cushion has been lost and the receiver has the advantage.

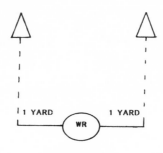

DIAGRAM 2-12

The receiver will usually make his deeper breaks between 10 and 14 yards downfield. The defender should maintain a cushion of three to four yards at the receiver's break point.

Horizontal position is also important when covering a receiver. Depending on the coverage call or field position, the defender should maintain good inside or outside position on his opponent. The good position a defensive back has will take one side away from the receiver, and, if he breaks away from the defender, he will cut into the area where the defender has help from another defensive player or the field boundaries.

A defender should take horizontal position on the receiver at alignment. His position should be one yard inside or outside his opponent's shoulder. He may take this position before the snap of the ball, or he should angle backpedal to his proper alignment as the ball is snapped. As the receiver attempts to stem to a position on the defender, he should angle backpedal, keeping the proper inside or outside leverage on his opponent. Proper concentration should be maintained throughout the route to a point downfield where the receiver reaches approximately 15 yards. At 15 yards the receiver usually will run his route without fighting for more position because of the timing factor between the quarterback and the receiver.

POSITION DRILLS

Drill #1: Mirror Drill

Purpose: To teach proper backpedalling technique along with the correct lateral and vertical cushion on a receiver.

Procedure: The defenders work in pairs. The two defensive backs align six to seven yards apart on the yard line. On command the receiver runs toward the defensive back moving laterally back and forth. The defender must backpedal and maintain proper cushion and inside or outside position. (See Diagram 2-13.)

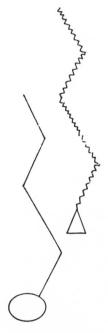

DIAGRAM 2-13

Coaching Points: It is important that the defender maintain his concentration and keep proper lateral position on the receiver. Begin the drill at half speed and work up to full speed. The defenders must backpedal at all times. They must not cross their feet and legs. The defensive back's hips and shoulders should mirror the receiver's. This is a good warm-up drill and should be used every day.

Drill #2: Corner Go

Purpose: To teach the defensive back the proper vertical and horizontal cushion in zone and man coverage against the Go route and when to come out of the backpedal.

Procedure: The defender should align six to seven yards deep and head up on the receiver. The coach will signal the receiver to run his Go route. On the Go route the receiver will work to get width toward the sideline as well as depth. The defensive back must mirror and get into crossover and run technique at the correct time. (See Diagram 2-14.)

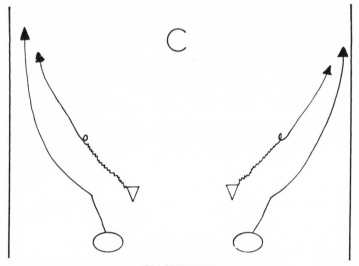

DIAGRAM 2-14

Coaching Points: It is important get an all-out effort from the receivers. The coach stands behind the defensive back in order to provide individual instructions. When working on man-to-man coverage, if the defensive back is stride for stride with the receiver and has contact with him he can turn inside to find the ball. If he is not in stride with the receiver he must sprint and stay turned to the receiver and read the receiver for the ball.

Drill #3: Cushion and Fake Drill

Purpose: There are two major fundamentals which are stressed in this drill. The player is taught the proper horizontal and vertical cushions that are necessary on a receiver and he is taught to ignore his opponent's first fake.

Procedure: The drill is run with the defender aligning himself six to seven yards from the receiver on his inside shoulder. On a command by the coach, the receiver sprints full speed to a point 15 yards from the line of scrimmage. When he reaches that point he will fake inside and run a Go or he will fake outside and run a Post pattern. The defender must backpedal and maintain proper cushion, ignore the first fake, then make the proper turn to defend the pattern. (See Diagram 2-15.)

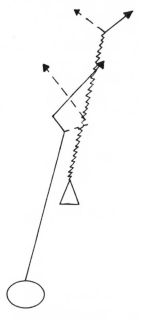

DIAGRAM 2-15

Coaching Points: As the receiver runs up the field, it is important for him to attempt to get to a head-up position before he makes his break at 15 yards. The coach should stand behind the defender to help him with proper cushion and turn techniques. The defensive back must learn to stay in his backpedal until the receiver has passed the 12- to 15-yard area from the line of scrimmage. He must also concentrate on not taking the first fake unless it is farther downfield than his 15-yard break area.

PLAYING THE BALL

The basic fundamental that separates the average defensive back from the great one is knowing where the ball is, and how to make the play on the ball once the pass is made. A common frustration of many coaches and players is having the defender in proper position on the receiver, but because he does not know where the ball is, he cannot properly react to intercept the ball or break up the pass.

When the ball is in the air, the defensive back should play the ball, not the receiver. When a defender plays a receiver instead of the ball he has no vision of where the football is and he cannot make a play on the ball. By seeing the football, the defensive back can break directly to the ball for the interception as if he were the intended receiver of the pass. The only exception to this rule is if the defender is forced to catch up with the receiver from behind. If he has to catch up, he should play the man's eyes and hands to get to the ball.

One should always play the ball at its highest point, using two hands. There will be times when the defensive back will not be able to get two hands on the ball and he will be forced to use one hand. When one hand is used there is a tendency to tip the ball. The defender should make sure that he knocks the ball down toward the ground.

It is important to develop a burst of speed to the ball once it is in the air. Five or six strides with quick recovery at near top speed is a tremendous advantage. Look through the receiver into the passer and play the ball aggressively.

INTERCEPTION

When a defensive back makes an interception he should attempt to make it above head level. If he takes it lower and waits for the ball, the receiver usually ends up making the catch. The defender should watch the interception into his hands and then put it away.

When making an interception in a crowd the defensive back should twist away from the receiver at the same time he is attempting to get the ball. The twisting motion gives additional force when the two players both have a hold on the football.

If there are two defenders covering one receiver, the one who is in position to intercept should yell the other defensive back off indicating he has the ball. The other defender should be right there and not let up. He should be ready for a deflected ball, block, or to help his teammate in any way. Using communication will minimize knocking each other off when going for the ball and will increase the chances for an interception.

After an interception the defensive back should go to the nearest sideline when returning the ball. His yardage will be greater by heading for the sideline rather than running straight upfield. Knowing that the interceptor will return the interception to the nearest sideline allows his teammates to block in the direction of his return. There are more offensive personnel in the middle of the field after a pass is thrown so returning the ball to the near sideline allows more opportunity to avoid potential tacklers. Usually the nearest receiver makes the tackle after an interception so the nearest defender should block back on the intended receiver.

INTERCEPTION DRILLS

Drill #1: Read and Break Drill

Purpose: To teach the defensive backs to read the head and shoulders of the thrower so that they can anticipate where the ball is going, thus enabling them to get a better break on the ball when it is thrown.

Procedure: To run the drill the coach aligns 10 to 15 yards from the defender in the middle of the hash marks. Two receivers are placed on the

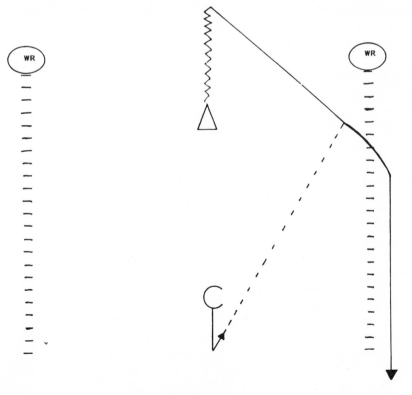

DIAGRAM 2-16

hash marks and the defender is located in the middle, three to four yards in front of them. When the coach steps back to simulate a pass, the defender begins to backpedal. The coach will turn his head and shoulders toward one receiver and throw the ball. The defensive back will break to the ball, intercept and sprint past the coach. The receivers are always stationary. (See Diagram 2-16.)

Coaching Points: As the coach begins his drop, the defender begins his backpedal and reads his head, eyes, shoulder and free arm. When the thrower's head and shoulder turn toward one receiver and the free arm comes off the ball, the defender breaks to the ball, intercepts and sprints past the coach.

It is important that the defender look the ball in to tuck it away. The defensive back has to secure the ball before he can score.

Drill #2: One-Man Comeback Drill

Purpose: To teach a defender to come back, or recover, on a ball that has been thrown a great distance.

Procedure: The defender is located seven yards from the coach. On the coach's command, the defensive back begins to backpedal. The defensive player should be allowed to backpedal eight to ten yards before the ball is thrown. The defender must plant his foot and drive forward, intercepting the football. The ball should be thrown in an area where the defender must come back to the ball. (See Diagram 2-17.)

DIAGRAM 2-17

Coaching Points: The defender must keep his forward lean and backpedal as quickly as possible with good arm motion. When the ball is thrown, the defender breaks with proper foot technique and sprints forward, making the interception. The ball should be intercepted at its highest point, then the defensive back should sprint past the coach.

Drill #3: Three-Man Comeback Drill

Purpose: To teach the defender to come back, or recover, on the ball at a great distance.

Procedure: Two corners and a safety split the field into thirds and line up seven yards from the coach. On the coach's command, the defensive backs begin backpedalling. The coach should allow the defenders to backpedal seven to ten yards and then throw the ball. The defensive back must plant his foot and drive forward intercepting the ball. The ball should be thrown in an area where the defensive back must come back to the ball. (See Diagram 2-18.)

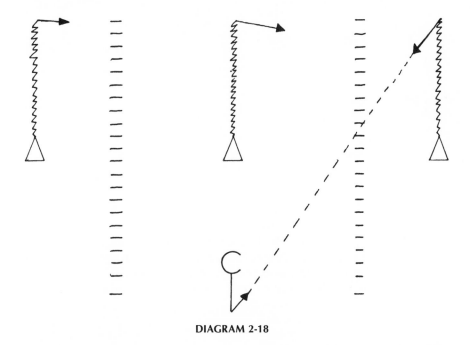

DIAGRAM 2-18

Coaching Points: The defender must keep low and use proper backpedal technique. All three defenders must break to the reception area. When the ball is intercepted at its highest point, all three players will sprint past the coach.

Drill #4: Backpedal Break to the Ball Drill

Purpose: To develop backpedalling skills, proper body position and weight distribution, plant and drive techniques and interception of the ball.

Procedure: The defender is located five to seven yards from the coach. On the coach's movement, the defender begins to backpedal. The defender is allowed to backpedal for 10 to 15 yards before the ball is thrown. The defensive back must plant, break to the ball for the interception, then sprint past the coach. (See Diagram 2-19.)

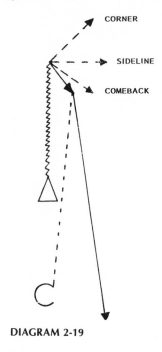

DIAGRAM 2-19

Coaching Points: The ball should be thrown in relation to the area in which specific routes would be run, such as a comeback, sideline or corner route. The player should use proper backpedal and plant technique. The defender reads the thrower and breaks for the interception, then sprints past the coach.

Drill #5: Two-on-One Drill

Purpose: To teach the defensive back that he can cover one-third area of responsibility. He is taught to maintain proper cushion on the receivers and also the proper angle for the interception point.

Procedure: Two receivers are placed on the hash marks. The coach takes a drop to simulate a pass while the receivers sprint up the hash mark, looking over their inside shoulder. (See Diagram 2-20.)

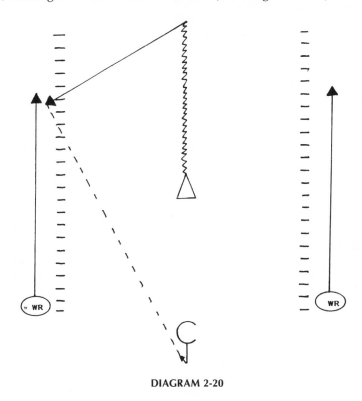

DIAGRAM 2-20

Coaching Points: The receivers will run straight upfield for 10 yards. The defensive back will backpedal and react to the ball. The defender should keep a five- to six-yard cushion and try to intercept the ball at its highest point.

Drill #6: Hash Mark Tip Drill

Purpose: To teach the defensive back to react to the ball thrown to the opposite side of the field and to make the interception on a tipped ball.

Procedure: Two receivers, one on each sideline, and two defenders, one on each hash mark at five yards deep, are placed to start this drill. On the coach's command the defenders backpedal for depth, keeping their five-yard cushion. As the coach steps to throw the ball, both defensive backs break to the ball. The first defender then tips the ball and the other one has to catch it in the air. Both defenders sprint past the coach on the sideline. (See Diagram 2-21.)

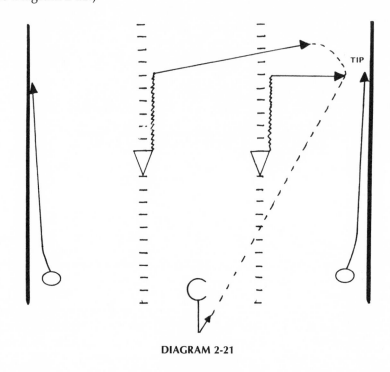

DIAGRAM 2-21

Coaching Points: The idea of never giving up on a thrown ball must be emphasized. When the head and shoulders of the thrower turn in the direction of the receiver, the defenders plant and break to the ball. The first defender must tip the ball high with both hands. The second defender intercepts the ball at the highest point and sprints by the coach. The ball should be tipped three to four yards from the sideline.

3

Tackling Techniques and Drills for Coaching the Defensive Back

A good defensive back should be skilled in the fundamentals and techniques of tackling. He should exhibit intensity and the desire to become a faultless tackler. Tackling fundamentals are a learned skill. Everyone can become a better tackler by concentrating and working on certain fundamentals.

A defender must always be under control and in good hitting position to be a good tackler. He must attack at nearly full speed and yet be under control. His knees should be partially flexed, back straight, eyes up and open, with the focus being through the opponent's far armpit.

On a straight-on tackle the defender should take away one side of the ball carrier and the contact point should be the eyes to the far armpit of his opponent. On an angle tackle, the eyes should be put on the opponent's far armpit, thus allowing his body to slide across the opponent and get added power. The defensive back should roll, or shoot, his hips upon contact. When the defender uses his hips he is using the strongest muscles in his body to his advantage. The tackler should throw his arms through and around his opponent and grab the jersey with his hands. He should keep his feet and legs driving upon contact, and always strive to knock the ball carrier backwards.

There are very few straight-on tackles made by defensive backs. The defender must learn to give the ball carrier only one way to go.

OPEN-FIELD TACKLING

The open-field tackle is a tackle that is made by the defensive back after the ball carrier has broken past the line of scrimmage and the defender is the only person between the runner and the goal line. The main objective of the open-field tackle is to get the ball carrier on the ground. The defensive back should not worry about how pretty the tackle is or if the runner gets a few extra yards after contact is made. This type of tackle is a game-saving tackle.

To execute the open-field tackle the defensive back, upon reading run, must squeeze down as much field as possible between the ball carrier and himself. When he gets to a cushion of approximately five yards from his opponent, he should come under control by bending his knees and lowering his body while maintaining good lateral balance, with his eyes focusing on the bottom of his opponent's numbers.

The defensive back should take a side away from the ball carrier so that he can anticipate the direction in which the runner will attempt to elude him. The defender's movement should be lateral, not forward. A forward, or lunging, action can result in a missed tackle because of improper balance. The proper lateral movement by the defender will allow a catching technique which will minimize the possibility of a missed tackle and a possible touchdown. Upon contact, the defensive back should get his eyes to the ball carrier's far armpit while wrapping and grabbing the opponent's jersey. He should keep his feet moving and if possible, keep his shoulders parallel with the line of scrimmage.

The open-field tackle is not a crushing, intimidating type of tackle, but a catching, sure type of touchdown-saving tackle.

TACKLING DRILLS

Drill #1: Tackling Sled Drill

Purpose: To teach proper tackling technique, use of the legs, arms, hips, shoulders and hands without using physical bodies as ball carriers.

DIAGRAM 3-1

Procedure: The defensive back should align seven to eight yards from the sled in good football position. On command, the defensive back sprints toward the sled with his body under control, tackles the sled, and drives it backwards in a straight line. (See Diagram 3-1.)

Coaching Points: The defender sprints to the sled with the proper base and body control, aiming at the middle of the pad. He should keep his shoulders square, hit with his eyes in the middle of the bag with his legs underneath him. The defender should bring his arms up as his hips rotate forward and lock his hand on his opposite wrist while keeping the feet driving. The sled should go backwards in a straight line.

Drill #2: Bag Drill

Purpose: To teach proper techniques and basic fundamentals of tackling. Proper "recovery" technique against a pass thrown to a receiver can be taught also.

Procedure: This drill is run by using one big bag held upright by the holder. The tackler attacks and tackles the bag with proper form. (See Diagram 3-2.)

DIAGRAM 3-2

Coaching Points: The defender's eyes are up and open and focused on the numbers on the bag. His contact point should drive into the middle of the bag and bring his arms up through it as he rolls his hips forward into the bag, locking his arms. The defensive back should keep his legs driving with a shoulder-width base and drive the bag backwards.

Drill #3: One-on-One Drill

Purpose: To emphasize good tackling form with a proper base, eyes open, arms out, explosion, locking of the hand and wrist, and follow-through of the hips.

Procedure: To start the drill, place two bell dummies five yards apart. The tackler, three yards from the ball carrier, faces the coach and on the command of "set" by the coach, both the tackler and the ball carrier run in place. On the command of "hit," the ball carrier moves forward in an upright position. The tackler makes a form tackle. (See Diagram 3-3.)

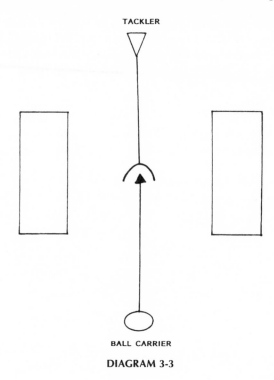

TACKLER

BALL CARRIER

DIAGRAM 3-3

Coaching Points: It is important to emphasize good tackling technique and proper stance. Correct aiming points such as eyes in the far armpit, movement of the feet and grabbing the back of the opponent's jersey with the hands should also be stressed.

Drill #4: Mirror Tackling Drill

Purpose: To emphasize quickness of feet, agility, maintaining proper relationship with the ball carrier, taking the proper pursuit angle and making a form tackle on a bell dummy.

Procedure: The drill begins by placing two bell dummies in a standing position 12 yards apart on a line. The tackler and the ball carrier align in the middle of the bags. The tackler is five yards from the line; the ball carrier aligns three yards from the line. On the command of "hit" by the coach, the ball carrier runs left and right several times; the tackler must mirror the ball carrier while maintaining a five-yard cushion from the line. On the second command, by whistle from the coach, the ball carrier sprints by one of the bell dummies. The tackler must sprint and have the proper angle to enable him to make the tackle at the location of the bell dummy. The tackler tackles the bell dummy, which is held up by players and is pushed forward as the tackler explodes. (See Diagram 3-4.)

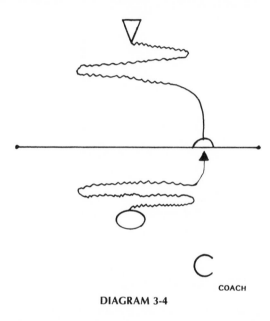

C

COACH

DIAGRAM 3-4

Coaching Points: The tackler must maintain a five-yard cushion from the line and mirror the ball carrier, not crossing his feet. He should take the proper angle and arrive at the dummy at the same time as the ball carrier. The ball carrier must sprint on the whistle to the bell dummy. The holders must offer resistance with the dummies.

Drill #5: Hash Tackling Drill

Purpose: To teach a defensive back to utilize the sideline, to force and contain the ball carrier, and to maintain the proper relationship so that the ball carrier cannot cut back against the grain.

Procedure: The coach should place one quarterback and ball carrier on the hash mark. The defender aligns on the opposite side. The quarterback can pitch the ball immediately to a running back or simulate the option play. The defensive back must square up, read, force, contain and tackle. (See Diagram 3-5.)

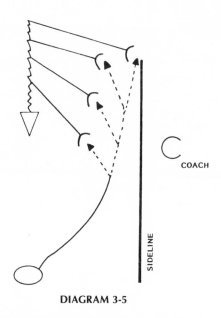

DIAGRAM 3-5

Coaching Points: The defender must keep his body under control. He should maintain a one-yard inside relationship on the ball carrier, therefore preventing the cut back. The defensive back should force the ball carrier to the sideline.

Drill #6: Ball Tackle Drill

Purpose: To teach the defender that he can make a sure tackle from a big cushion.

Procedure: The defensive back is located seven yards from the receiver at a midpoint of the middle one-third. The coach is located on the hash

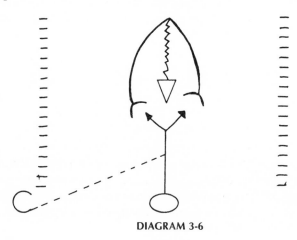

DIAGRAM 3-6

mark. On command, the receiver runs forward; the defender maintains a five-yard vertical cushion. The coach throws to the receiver, who can make a move in any direction. The defender must recover, break down, and make a sure tackle. (See Diagram 3-6.)

Coaching Points: The defender must maintain a five-yard vertical cushion while looking at the coach. The defensive back must break down in good hitting position with his feet moving.

Drill #7: Side Tackling Drill

Purpose: To teach the defensive back to sprint, come under control at three to four yards from the ball carrier and execute a form tackle, hitting on the rise.

Procedure: The coach should locate the defensive back 10 yards from a line facing a ball carrier who also is 10 yards from the same line. On the command of "hit," the ball carrier and tackler sprint directly toward one another. The ball carrier sprints to the line and breaks at a 90-degree angle left or right. The tackler sprints hard for seven yards, comes under control at three yards from the ball carrier, and executes a form tackle on the ball carrier. (See Diagram 3-7.)

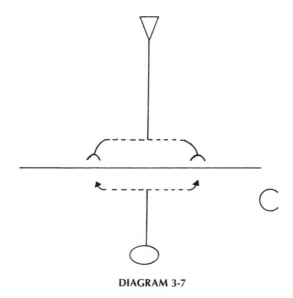

DIAGRAM 3-7

Coaching Points: The tackler must read the belt buckle of the ball carrier. The tackler must get under control at three yards from the ball carrier. He should emphasize a good base with his feet moving. As the ball carrier makes his break, the tackler explodes and executes a form tackle. The ball carrier should never cross the line.

Drill #8: Moving One-on-One Drill

Purpose: The purpose of this drill is the same as the One-on-One Drill, except the defensive back will shuffle laterally before making the tackle.

Procedure: Two bell dummies are placed five yards apart. The tackler is positioned three yards from the ball carrier, facing him. On the command of "set" by the coach, both the tackler and the ball carrier run in place. On the command of "hit," the ball carrier moves forward in an upright position. The tackler makes a form tackle. (See Diagram 3-8.)

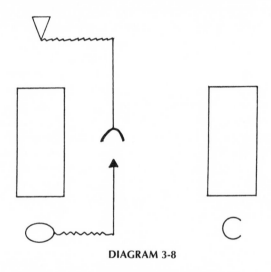

DIAGRAM 3-8

Coaching Points: The coach should emphasize that the tackler should get his eyes on the ball carrier's far armpit. He should also emphasize the explosion on the tackler's hips, along with the wrapping of the arms and gripping the ball carrier's jersey.

Drill #9: Butt Drills

Purpose: To teach explosion and proper location of the eyes and use of the arms, hips and legs in tackling.

Procedure: Two defensive players are lined up in a two-point "hitting position" inside a five-yard area on a line. Place a ball carrier one yard across the line. On a "set" command the two defensive players start moving their feet in short choppy steps. On a "go" command the offensive player tries to cross the line. The defensive players, keeping their shoulders square, shuffle with the ball carrier in a low hitting position. As the ball carrier tries to cross the line, the defensive player explodes into the ball carrier with his eyes aiming at the far armpit, emphasizing hitting with his legs under him, being under control, eyes and arms coming, and not overextending and going across the line. The ball carrier, going at about three-fourths speed, and only one yard from the line, then challenges the other defender. Each defender should get two hits at the ball carrier. (See Diagram 3-9.)

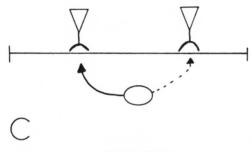

DIAGRAM 3-9

Coaching Points: Players should be in a low hitting position moving with shoulders parallel to the line. The defenders should explode into the ball carrier with the eyes focusing in an upward direction. The defender should extend his legs fully and bring his hips through, looking up with his eyes and making certain they are open.

4

Basic Selected Coverages

All pass coverages for the defensive backfield are a combination of five basic coverages. The techniques and strategies found in Three-Deep Zone, Two-Deep Zone, Two-Deep Man Under, Man Free and Blitz are common in any coverage a coach can devise.

Coaches can combine any parts of the coverages to create another coverage, but the techniques remain consistent. It is important for the defensive back to perfect and master these specific techniques in order to properly execute the coverage and perform to his best potential.

THREE-DEEP ZONE

Three-Deep Zone is a coverage that divides the field into four equal zones extending from the line of scrimmage to a distance of 12 to 15 yards into the secondary. Three-Deep Zones extend from the depth of the underneath zones at 12 to 18 yards to a point that reaches into the secondary to the opponent's goal line, or as deep as the deepest receiver runs his route.

Defenders executing the Three-Deep Zone will drop to their designated zones and defend the opponent, or opponents, who are in their zone when the ball is released by the quarterback. It is important that a defender not chase receivers in his zone until the ball is released. The defensive player must always know where the ball is and get a great break on the ball when it is released.

Three-Deep Zone is a good sound coverage for defending deep or crossing offensive pass routes. This coverage is effective against the long pass because the deep zone players should always be as deep as the deepest threatening patterns.

Zone defenses are usually easier to learn because the defenders will have an area to defend instead of an individual receiver. Also, the defender can normally read whether the play is a run or a pass much more quickly because he can see the total picture in front of him and not focus on just one receiver. When playing a team that has your defensive backfield mismatched in talent, the zone concept will be more advantageous.

COVERAGE: THREE-DEEP ZONE VS PRO SET

PLAYER	ALIGNMENT	KEY	PASS RESPONSIBILITY	RUN RESPONSIBILITY
MAC	FRONT CALLED	OG/NB	HOOK/CURL	FRONT CALLED
WILL	FRONT CALLED	OG/NB	HOOK/CURL	FRONT CALLED
DEUCE CORNER	9:1	QB	DEEP OUTSIDE 1/3	TO: SECONDARY SUPPORT AWAY: BACKSIDE PURSUIT
STRONG SAFETY	5:4	TE/QB	CURL/FLAT	TO: PRIMARY FORCE AWAY: FOLD
FREE SAFETY	12 YDS MIDDLE OF FIELD	QB	MIDDLE 1/3	ALLEY
OUTSIDE LINEBACKER	5:4	QB	CURL/FLAT	TO: PRIMARY FORCE AWAY: FOLD
ACE CORNER	9:1	QB	DEEP OUTSIDE 1/3	TO: PRIMARY FORCE AWAY: BACKSIDE PURSUIT

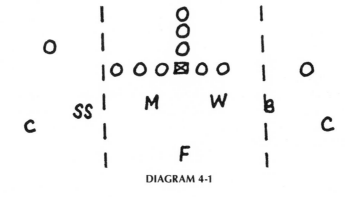

DIAGRAM 4-1

Three-Deep Zone is also a good coverage for strongside run support. However, weakside run support, along with passes that attack the seams of the zones, can give this coverage problems. The pass completion percentage is usually higher when playing zone coverages. (See Diagram 4-1.)

TWO-DEEP ZONE

Two-Deep Zone is a coverage which utilizes five zones extending from the line of scrimmage to a distance of 12 to 15 yards into the defensive backfield. The area beyond the underneath five zones is divided into two equal deep zones which extend to the opponent's goal line.

At the snap of the ball the defenders will drop to their appropriate zones and break to the football upon release of the ball. The defensive player must not chase receivers through his zone and must break to the football as it is thrown.

Defenders must see the quarterback at all times, and must watch the receivers with their peripheral vision. They must study the quarterback's release, as that is the most important aspect involved in breaking to the football and making a play on the ball.

Two-Deep Zone coverage is excellent against offensive teams who throw to the flats or underneath crossing patterns. Run support is very good on both sides of the formation because of the corner support.

Two-Deep Zone is also an excellent coverage to take away the out pattern. It is one of the best coverages to disrupt receivers' patterns. The corners and linebackers can jam receivers and then proceed to their pass defense areas comfortably because they have two half-field safeties covering on top of them.

Deep seam patterns are very effective when attacking the Two-Deep Zone coverage. (See Diagram 4-2.)

TWO-DEEP MAN UNDER

Two-Deep Man Under is a very good pass coverage because it allows the defensive team to Man up all of the eligible receivers and play Two-Deep Zone on top of the formation. This strategy basically gives the defense the ability to cover each offensive receiver with one and one-half defensive players.

The Two-Deep Man Under coverage takes away the underneath routes by playing Man on each receiver. When the receiver goes deep he is double covered because he has a man on him with a safety playing zone on top. When the ball is released, the safety on top will break to the football.

COVERAGE: TWO-DEEP ZONE VS PRO SET

PLAYER	ALIGNMENT	KEY	PASS RESPONSIBILITY	RUN RESPONSIBILITY
MAC	FRONT CALLED	OG/NB	HOOK	FRONT CALLED
WILL	FRONT CALLED	OG/NB	HOOK/CURL	FRONT CALLED
DEUCE CORNER	6 YDS HEAD UP	QB	1. DISRUPT ROUTE OF #1 2. FLAT	PRIMARY FORCE
OUTSIDE LINEBACKER	1:1	TE/QB	CURL	ALLEY
FREE SAFETY	12/14 ON HASH	#1 TO QB	1/2 ZONE; READ JAM 1. #1 INSIDE RELEASE; SHUFFLE 2. #1 OUTSIDE RELEASE; BACKPEDAL ON HASH	SECONDARY SUPPORT
STRONG SAFETY	12/14 ON HASH	#1 TO QB	1/2 ZONE; READ JAM 1. #1 INSIDE RELEASE; SHUFFLE 2. #1 OUTSIDE RELEASE; BACKPEDAL ON HASH	SECONDARY SUPPORT
ACE CORNER	6 YDS HEAD UP	QB	1. DISRUPT ROUTE OF #1 2. FLAT	PRIMARY FORCE
SIX	----------------------------	-----------	SAME AS WILL LINEBACKER	----------------------------

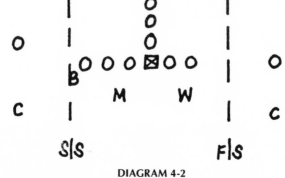

DIAGRAM 4-2

This coverage is excellent when defending most pass patterns. However, a team that picks or blocks a defender when he runs a route has success versus the Man Under concept. Even though picks are illegal in football, officials rarely call them during a game. Run support is also very weak when using the Two-Deep Man Under coverage. (See Diagram 4-3.)

COVERAGE: TWO-DEEP MAN UNDER VS PRO SET

PLAYER	ALIGNMENT	KEY	PASS RESPONSIBILITY	RUN RESPONSIBILITY
MAC	FRONT CALLED	GD/NB	COVER OWN BACK	FRONT CALLED
WILL	FRONT CALLED	GD/NB	COVER OWN BACK	FRONT CALLED
DEUCE CORNER	PRESS	#1	#1 M/M	M/M
OUTSIDE LINEBACKER	PRESS	#2	M/M ON #2	M/M
FREE SAFETY	12/14 HASH	QB	1/2 ZONE	TO: FORCE AWAY: ALLEY
STRONG SAFETY	---- SAME AS FREE ----			
ACE CORNER	---- SAME AS DEUCE ----			

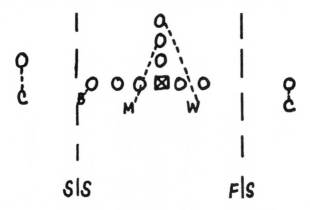

DIAGRAM 4-3

COVERAGE: MAN FREE VS PRO SET

PLAYER	ALIGNMENT	KEY	PASS RESPONSIBILITY	RUN RESPONSIBILITY
MAC	FRONT CALLED	OG/NB	1. COVER OWN BACK 2. POSSIBLE TEAMWORK WITH STRONG SAFETY	FRONT CALLED
WILL	FRONT CALLED	OG/NB	1. COVER OWN BACK 2. POSSIBLE TEAMWORK WITH OUTSIDE LINEBACKER	FRONT CALLED
DEUCE CORNER	6 YDS TO PRESS: INSIDE 1 YD	#1	#1 M/M	M/M
STRONG SAFETY	7 YDS TO PRESS OUTSIDE #2	#2	1. #2 M/M 2. POSSIBLE TEAMWORK WITH MAC	M/M
FREE SAFETY	12 YDS MIDDLE OF FIELD	QB	FREE	ALLEY
OUTSIDE LINEBACKER	VARIED	QB	1. FREE 2. POSSIBLE TEAMWORK WITH WILL	ALLEY
ACE CORNER	6 YDS TO PRESS: INSIDE 1 YD	#1	#1 M/M	M/M

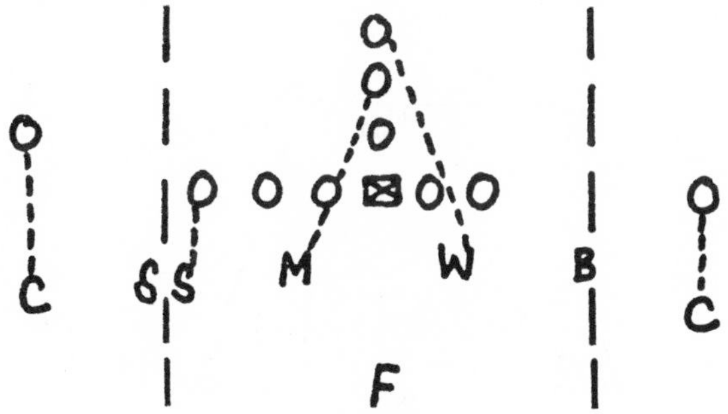

DIAGRAM 4-4

MAN FREE

Man Free is a coverage which plays man-to-man on all of the offensive receivers, and has a free safety who is playing deep zone on top of the formation. This is a good pass defense as all receivers are covered by man-to-man with a safety covering for any deep passing threat. Man Free is better against the run, but it is vulnerable to pick plays and screens. (See Diagram 4-4.)

BLITZ COVERAGE

Blitz coverage is used when a team is blitzing six to seven defenders. When a team blitzes so many defenders, the secondary must play man-to-

COVERAGE:			BLITZ	
PLAYER	ALIGNMENT	KEY	PASS RESPONSIBILITY	RUN RESPONSIBILITY
MAC	A-GAP	BALL	DOG	
WILL	B-GAP	BALL	DOG	
DEUCE CORNER	PRESS: 6	#1	M/M	M/M
STRONG SAFETY	D-GAP	BALL	BLITZ WITH PEEL	M/M
FREE SAFETY	PRESS: 6	#2	#2 MAN-TO-MAN	M/M
LINEBACKER	D-GAP	BALL	BLITZ WITH PEEL	M/M
ACE CORNER	PRESS: 6	#1	M/M	M/M
SIX	B-GAP	BALL	DOG	

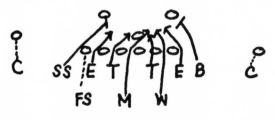

DIAGRAM 4-5

man on the four primary receivers with a linebacker playing man-to-man on the remaining back.

Blitzing a team can make the big play happen for the defense. It may cause a sack or an offensive mistake which could lead to a fumble or interception. If the Blitz does not get to the quarterback quickly, the defensive backs are at a disadvantage because they are playing man-to-man with no linebacker support on the coverage. Screens and receiver mismatches neutralize the strategy of blitzing. (See Diagram 4-5.)

A defensive cornerback's technique must be highly consistent in order to execute the five previously discussed coverages. The cornerback techniques discussed in the next chapter are specific to these five coverages, or any combination a coach may choose to utilize.

5

Techniques and Drills for Teaching the Corner to Execute Selected Basic Coverages

JAM TECHNIQUE

The Jam technique is one of the most important techniques a corner must master when his responsibility is to roll up to defend the flat or when it is a pass play, such as in Two-Deep Zone. At the snap of the football, the corner's alignment should be five to six yards deep and head up on the receiver with his outside foot up.

The defender's key should be the quarterback. If the quarterback comes straight down the line of scrimmage, as when running an option play, the corner will contain the football and take the pitch man on the option play.

If the quarterback comes off the line of scrimmage, the cornerback will execute the Jam technique. The corner will step up with his inside foot to parallel his stance. He focuses his eyes on the lower part of his opponent's jersey number. The defensive back will not lunge, or go forward, but will go laterally, not breaking the parallel angle. He should be in a low athletic stance with his elbows in to his sides and the palms of his hands facing the receiver.

It is important for the defensive back to work his feet laterally so that he can get solid contact on his opponent. The speed of the receiver should actually give the defensive back his power when jamming the receiver. The shoulders should be kept square with the line of scrimmage when making contact. The defender's eyes should stay on the opponent's numbers until contact is made.

The most common mistake a defensive back makes, besides not moving his feet laterally, is trying to sneak a quick peek inside to see the play before he makes contact. When contact is made, the defender's main objective is to disrupt the receiver's route. It will not matter if the receiver goes outside the jam or inside. If the cornerback has good position on the receiver he may use a six-inch jab with his hands. (See Diagram 5-1.)

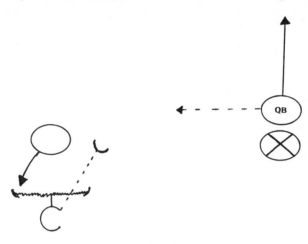

DIAGRAM 5-1

When contact is made the defender may take a look inside to search for the inside receiver who may be threatening the flat area. He must maintain contact with his opponent when searching the inside.

It is important to maintain contact as long as possible with the receiver. If the receiver is releasing inside, the corner should stay with that receiver as long as he is not threatened by the inside receiver who is invading the corner's flat responsibility.

The corner will also release the receiver when his opponent reaches a point on the field even with his position. The defensive back will then "Z" back to the hole, which is an area 10 to 12 yards deep between the sideline and the field number. (See Diagram 5-2.)

The technique of "Z-ing" back to the hole will put the defensive back in a position to handle his flat responsibilities and also help the safety by being under a pattern which is thrown to the hole. This position forces the quarterback to throw the ball over the corner, which allows the safety a better break on the football. If the quarterback throws to the flat, he can break to his flat responsibility.

The corner may either backpedal to the hole, or use a crossover step.

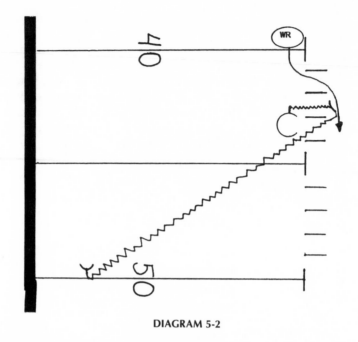

DIAGRAM 5-2

He must always be looking back inside to search for the inside receiver threatening his area of responsibility.

   If the receiver releases outside, the corner must utilize the same technique as if he releases inside. The defensive back tries to jam the receiver out of bounds if he can. When the corner's shoulders start to turn he must release the receiver and turn inside, then run to a point 10 to 12 yards upfield getting to the field numbers. (See Diagram 5-3.)

   The technique of running to the numbers after the jam helps the safety's play on the fade route. The corner's position makes the quarterback throw the ball over the corner, which keeps the ball in the air longer, thus allowing the safety more time to get to the football for the interception. If the quarterback throws to the flat, the corner is in excellent position to react to his responsibility.

TRAIL TECHNIQUE

   The Trail technique is performed when a corner has man-to-man responsibility on his receiver and the safeties are helping him by playing zone over the top of him. When executing a coverage such as Two-Deep Man, the corner is only responsible for the pass. He has no run responsibilities.

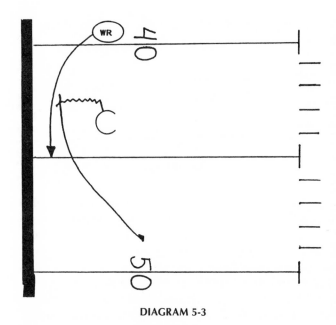

DIAGRAM 5-3

The defensive back will align himself at the line of scrimmage in a bump-and-run position. He will straddle the receiver's inside foot with his inside foot in a toe-to-instep relationship. The most important factor is to not let the receiver get to the defensive back's inside. If the receiver tries to release inside, the corner will jam him into the backfield, thus eliminating the threat of a pick play, or a crack-back block on a running play. When the Trail technique is used versus the inside release, the inside foot should never be moved. The defensive back should concentrate on the bottom of the inside number. (See Diagram 5-4.)

If the receiver releases outside, it is important not to move the inside foot until the receiver is parallel with the defensive back, or has taken his second step. The cornerback must be patient. He must ignore all outside moves by the receiver. The cornerback must realize that he has safety help on top and that he is his own underneath coverage.

When the receiver releases outside, the corner will trail him by one

DIAGRAM 5-4

stride. He will align himself straddling the inside leg of one invisible man inside of the receiver. (See Diagram 5-5.)

DIAGRAM 5-5

The corner will concentrate on the lower inside number of the receiver. He will trail the receiver, without fully extending his body. When the receiver's numbers come up, it is the corner's key that the receiver is getting himself in position to make his break on the route. At this point, the defensive back should run in a semi-crouch, thus allowing more balance as he prepares to defend the receiver's break.

The defensive back must ignore all outside breaking routes by his opponent. The angle and distance of the throw when defending an outside break by the receiver allow the defensive back to rally to a point underneath and between the receiver and quarterback and make the play on the football. (See Diagram 5-6.)

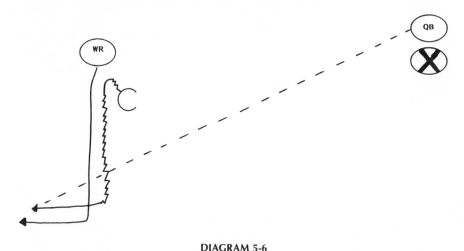

DIAGRAM 5-6

When the receiver makes an inside breaking pattern, the defensive back is in excellent inside position to defend the route. It is important for

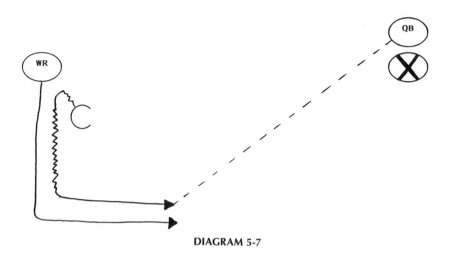

DIAGRAM 5-7

the corner to get between the receiver and quarterback, thus making it impossible for the offense to execute the play. (See Diagram 5-7.)

The defender must keep his eye contact on the receiver well into his break. If the defensive back looks back to the quarterback on the inside break, he can lose the receiver on an in and out route, or a post route. (See Diagrams 5-8 through 5-11.)

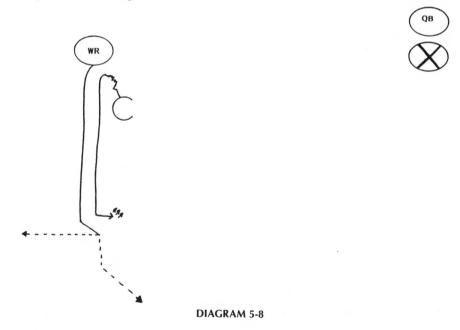

DIAGRAM 5-8

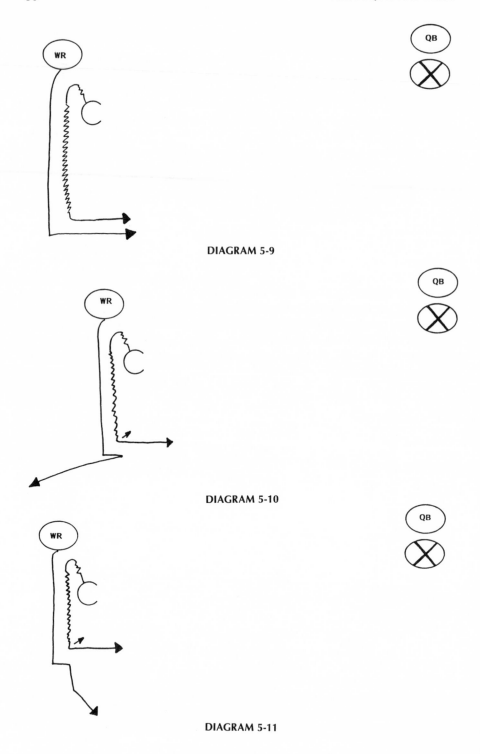

DIAGRAM 5-9

DIAGRAM 5-10

DIAGRAM 5-11

ALIGNMENT TECHNIQUE

Proper alignment is one of the most crucial aspects of playing the defensive back position. The defender must have correct depth and width from a receiver. The corner's depth yardage will vary depending on his responsibility in a given coverage call. Depth will vary from the defensive back being on the line of scrimmage when using a coverage that utilizes the Trail technque, to seven to ten yards deep when his responsibility is defending the deep one-third zone or when playing man coverage.

Width alignment is very important to maintain because a good receiver will always work on getting a head-up position on a defensive back. The defender must maintain his width alignment throughout the pass route.

When lining up on a receiver's inside, the defender should visualize an imaginary man on the inside of the opponent. If he aligns on the outside of his opponent, he should use the same visualization of an imaginary player on the receiver's outside. If taking away the inside shade of the receiver, the defensive back should straddle the inside foot of the imaginary player. If he wants to shade the outside of the receiver, he should straddle the outside foot of the imaginary receiver. (See Diagram 5-12.)

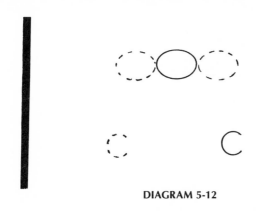

DIAGRAM 5-12

STREAK TECHNIQUE

Whether a corner is playing deep one-third zone or man-to-man with no safety help, he must perfect the Streak technique. The receiver will usually stem toward the sideline when running a streak route. He will also give an indication of running the streak by not raising his numbers throughout his route.

When the defender reads the streak keys, he must come out of his backpedal and step with an outside foot step that strides upfield. The defensive back has to open his hips and not be extended to allow his body to proceed upfield with as little effort and as quickly as possible.

The defensive back should run stride for stride with the receiver, looking him in the eye. As he runs with the receiver, he should try to squeeze him out of bounds. This technique is continued until the receiver's eyes show that he is going to catch the ball and his hands go up to make the catch. At this point in time the defensive back will turn his head into the field to look for the football. It is very important for the defender to keep his shoulders pointing up the football field when he turns his head. A defender will run in the direction his shoulders are pointed. (See Diagram 5-13.)

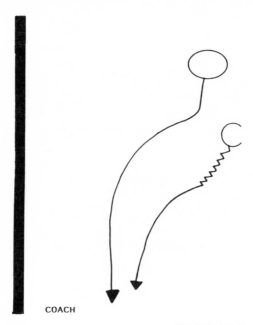

COACH

DIAGRAM 5-13

When a defender is behind a receiver while defending a streak pattern, he should never look for the ball. He will catch up with the receiver and strip the ball by putting his hands in the receiver's hands, therefore making it impossible to catch the ball. The defensive back should also not look for the ball when it is thrown on a quick streak, such as in a goal-line situation, or on a Blitz. In these two situations the ball is thrown too quickly and it is better to play the receiver's hands. The Streak, or Go, Drill is discussed in Chapter 2.

CLOSE THE POST TECHNIQUE

The corner uses the Close the Post technique when he defends the outside one-third responsibility of Three-Deep Zone. When the receiver runs a post pattern in the defensive back's zone, he must close the post so he can make the play if the ball is thrown on the post break. The defender must also Close the Post so the receiver cannot run a post flag route without running through the defensive back. This will give the defender good position when defending the flag pattern.

Close the Post is performed by the defender drifting in the direction of the post break while calling out the route to the free safety. After closing the post he should get depth in his zone and watch for a threatening combination pattern. (See Diagram 5-14.)

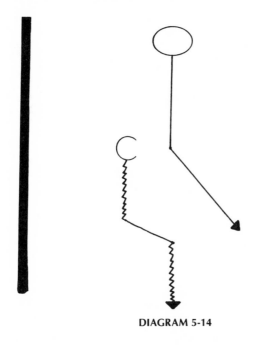

DIAGRAM 5-14

POST FLAG TECHNIQUE

When defending the Post Flag pattern, whether the defense is zone or man coverage, the defender should give up body position for a smoother foot pattern. The defensive back will first Close the Post and keep his body in a position that forces the receiver to run through the defender if he is attempting to run a flag pattern. When the flag aspect of the pass route is run by the receiver, the defender should not drop step, but should mirror the receiver, which puts the defender in a position between the receiver and the sideline. The drop step takes too much time to perform and sometimes trips the defender. (See Diagram 5-15.)

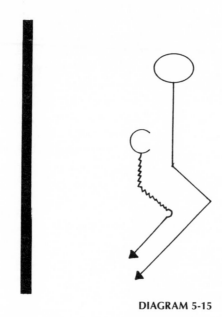

DIAGRAM 5-15

SIDELINE AND GO TECHNIQUE

When playing man-to-man coverage on any sideline pattern, a defensive back should break toward the shoulder closest to the sideline. The defender's cushion from the receiver should allow for the possibility of a streak break off of the original pattern. It is important for the defender to use the Sideline and Go read technique, which is to key the receiver's numbers. If the receiver turns the numbers on his back to the defensive back, he is getting in position to catch the football on a sideline pattern. If the receiver does not show his back numbers to the defensive back on his sideline break, he is keeping his body in position to run a Sideline and Go pattern. If the defender does make a mistake and plays the sideline pattern too tight and the receiver breaks on a streak pattern, the defender must attempt to knock the receiver down, or out of bounds. (See Diagram 5-16.)

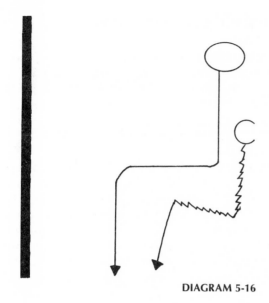

DIAGRAM 5-16

STRIPPING THE BALL TECHNIQUE

Many times the receiver runs a perfect pattern and has good position on the defender to catch the football. When an offensive play is well executed and the receiver is in possession of the ball, the defender must attempt to strip it from his opponent.

The Strip technique is performed in two almost simultaneous actions. The Rip is performed by stripping the ball with the defender's arm that is closest to the quarterback. This, hopefully, will shake the ball loose from the receiver. The second phase of the football strip technique is called the Club and happens at almost the exact moment of the Rip. The Club is simply as it states, the defender clubs the receiver's helmet with his off arm. The philosophy behind the Club technique is that most coaches have taught the receiver to keep his "eye on the ball" when catching the football. The Club is used to take the receiver's eye off the football. The defensive back must be going for the ball to make the play on the ball for the tackle to be a legal play.

When executing the Strip technique it is important for the defender to throw his hips into the receiver for added momentum. It is also necessary to always keep the defensive back's body in a position between the receiver and the goal line so he does not miss the tackle and give up a big play.

PRESS TECHNIQUE (BUMP AND RUN)

When a Blitzing strategy is used to attack an offense with six or more pass rushers, a defensive back must play his receiver one-on-one with no help from other defenders. The defender can align off the receiver or he may choose to press, or align himself on the line of scrimmage. If he lines up on the receiver, he must never let the offensive player get inside of him. He should straddle the receiver's inside foot and jam the man back into the backfield if the offensive man releases inside.

On the receiver's first movement, the defender will punch with both hands at the bottom of the opponent's numbers. It is important that he keep his thumbs up, which will keep the elbows close to his side. The defender must not overextend or lose his balance when executing the punch technique. By using the punch technique the defensive player will jam the receiver into the backfield if he releases inside. If the receiver releases outside, the defensive back will widen his route and, therefore, destroy the timing of the route execution between the quarterback and receiver.

If a receiver runs a Go or Streak route, the defensive back will widen the route, making sure the offensive man cannot come back inside, and will then get in a position on the inside hip of the receiver and try to snuggle him out of bounds.

The defensive back will run stride for stride on the Go route and will keep his eyes on the receiver until his hands reach for the ball and then the defender will put his hands in the receiver's hands and slap the ball away.

If the Blitz is executed successfully the ball will be thrown quickly, which does not allow the defender time to look for the football. Many times just disrupting the route and the timing of the offensive play will allow the Blitz to be successful. A coach cannot live with the Blitz unless he has two outstanding corners who can play tough man-to-man defense. (See Diagram 5-17.)

The techniques and drills discussed in this chapter will be of great value when teaching a defensive back to execute the strategies of the defensive backfield to the maximum.

TECHNIQUE DRILLS

Drill #1: Press (Bump-and-Run) Drill

Purpose: To teach alignment, Punch technique and position of a corner who is in a one-on-one press alignment on a receiver. Through repetition the defender learns the importance of balance and reaction time when playing Bump-and-Run technique.

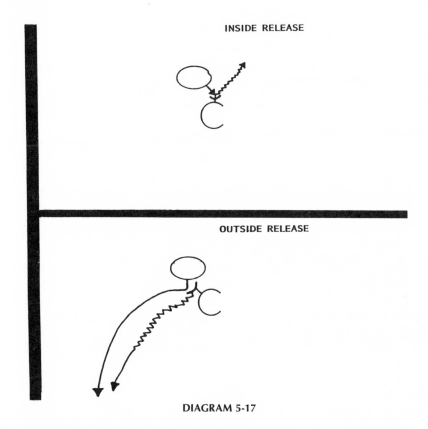

INSIDE RELEASE

OUTSIDE RELEASE

DIAGRAM 5-17

Procedure: A defender will be in a press position on the next man in line, who is acting as a receiver. The drill is broken down to first work several repetitions on the Punch technique, getting the defender to be in proper alignment, straddling the receiver's inside foot while maintaining a good football stance. The defender's outside foot can be back, but it should not be back more than the inside heel.

After several repetitions of the Punch technique the receiver will start releasing inside and outside on the coach's direction. When the receiver releases inside, the defensive back will jam him into the backfield so that it is impossible to pick another defender on a pass, or block him if it was a running play. When the receiver releases outside, the defender will punch and widen the opponent so the timing of the route will be destroyed.

Coaching Points: It is important to have total concentration during this drill. The defender must not overextend when executing the Punch technique. The defensive back must maintain his balance throughout the technique as the defender must use his total athletic profile to maintain tight coverage on the receiver. The coach can break this drill down by having the players work in pairs so they can work together on each phase of the technique. The main factor in teaching the Bump-and-Run technique is to allow the defensive backs as many repetitions as possible. (See Diagram 5-18.)

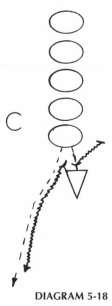

DIAGRAM 5-18

Drill #2: Jam Drill

Purpose: To teach the defensive back the first stage of the Jam technique.

Procedure: As previously discussed in this chapter, when a cornerback is in a coverage where he is rolled up and responsible for the flat zone, he must perfect the Jam technique. From a good football stance with the corner's outside foot up at a five-yard depth, the first key is on the quarterback. When the quarterback comes off the line of scrimmage, the defensive back steps up with his inside foot, focuses on the receiver and executes the Jam technique.

Divide the defensive backs in half and place in two lines. Each defensive back will rotate from simulating the receiver to executing the defensive back's responsibilities. If the drill is slowed down to better emphasize the finer points of the technique, it will allow the coach the opportunity to teach and demonstrate to each individual player. The drill is stopped at the point of contact between the two athletes. (See Diagram 5-19.)

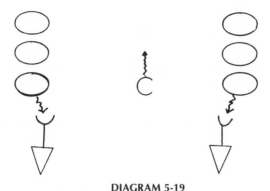

DIAGRAM 5-19

Coaching Points: When performing the drill it is important to start with a good stance and read the quarterback's key. As the quarterback comes off the line, the defensive back must maintain a five-yard depth and move laterally. The defensive back's eyes focus on the lower part of the opponent's jersey numbers. At the point of contact, the defensive back continues to maintain hand contact while working the receiver laterally. When the defensive back has secured the receiver, he will look inside to search for the inside receiver. The drill is stopped by a whistle before separation of the two athletes.

The drill is run more efficiently when the receiver uses one of the defensive back's outside shoulders as a point of aim and runs at three-fourths speed. This allows better emphasis to teach the contact point of the Jam technique. The defender must disrupt the receiver's route in either direction.

Drill #3: Jam-Z Back to Hole

Purpose: To teach the defensive back the technique of jamming the receiver inside and then getting himself into an area called the hole, which is approximately 12 yards deep in the secondary and five yards inside the sideline.

Procedure: The corner gets to the hole to force the quarterback to throw the ball over him, therefore allowing the safety to get a better break on the ball. If the quarterback throws to the flat, the defensive back is in good position to rally to his flat responsibility.

This drill is set up exactly like the previous Jam Drill with the exception of the quarterback throwing the ball to the corner when he gets to the hole. (See Diagram 5-20.)

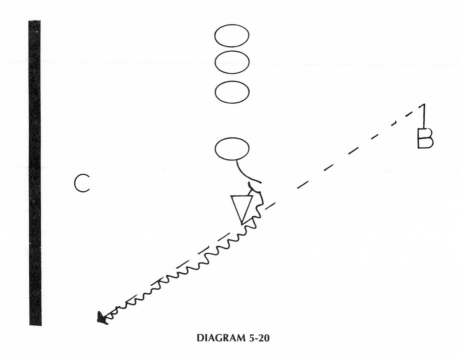

DIAGRAM 5-20

Coaching Points: When teaching this drill it is important to emphasize the Jam technique and search for the inside receiver first. At a later time a coach can add a back coming out of the backfield.

If the Jam inside does not take the defensive back too far away from the sideline, he can backpedal to the hole. If there is a short split by the receiver and the defensive back is farther away from the sideline, he may want to use a crossover step, but must always be looking inside.

When the defensive back gets to the hole, he should be in a shuffle to lower his body so he can get a good break on the football. The corner should always take away the intermediate pass and rally to the short pass. He must not jump his flat responsibility until the ball is thrown there.

Drill #4: Jam Drill—Run to the Numbers

Purpose: To teach the cornerback to jam the receiver and then get into a position between the quarterback and receiver, thus making a pass completion difficult.

Procedure: The Jam and Run to the Numbers Drill is coached the same way as the Jam-Z to the Hole Drill, with the exception that the receiver stems outside on his release. The quarterback will throw to the defensive back when he runs to the numbers on the field. (See Diagram 5-21.)

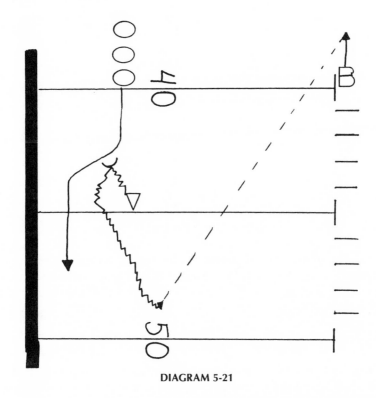

DIAGRAM 5-21

Coaching Points: It is important to teach the defensive back to maintain contact on the Jam. When his shoulders start to turn toward the sideline, he must turn back inside and run to the field numbers. The defensive back must not turn his back to the quarterback.

A common problem when teaching this technique is the defensive back can get too deep when running to the numbers. The corner must not run beyond 10 to 12 yards before he gets into his shuffle.

Drill #5: Trail Drill—Inside Release

Purpose: To teach the defensive back the importance of never allowing a receiver to release inside.

Procedure: Under no circumstances should a defensive back ever allow a receiver to release inside. To emphasize this, the Inside Release Drill is the first drill taught when teaching the Trail technique. The drill is set up by positioning a line of receivers across from a line of defensive backs and giving a starting count for the drill to begin. (See Diagram 5-22.)

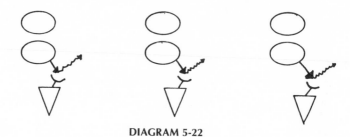

DIAGRAM 5-22

Coaching Points: The first emphasis of this drill must be assuring a proper stance by the defensive back. The defender should straddle the inside foot of the receiver. The feet should be slightly staggered with the inside foot up in a toe-to-instep relationship. The defensive back's eyes must focus on the inside number of the receiver's jersey. When the defensive back starts making good contact on the inside release and pushing the receiver back in the backfield the coach may add an outside fake, then an inside release to the drill. It should be emphasized that the defensive back should not move his inside foot on the first outside move by the receiver.

Drill #6: Trail Drill—Outside Break

Purpose: To teach the defensive back to trail the receiver so that he is between the quarterback and receiver, thus making a pass completion difficult.

Procedure: The Trail Drill—Outside Break begins with a line of defensive backs and one line of receivers. This drill also utilizes a quarterback who throws the interception to the defensive back at the conclusion of the drill. The defender will move on the receiver's movement. The receiver will release outside and run a 15-yard sideline pattern. (See Diagram 5-23.)

Coaching Points: When the receiver releases outside, it is important for the defensive back not to get too physical with him because he may push the receiver further away, making it more difficult to defend him.

The Trail alignment must be one stride behind the receiver and one invisible man inside the receiver. The defender must not follow too closely or he will overrun the receiver's break. The defensive back must ignore all outside breaks because he has the time and angle to rally under the receiver's pattern to make the play.

When the defensive back trails the receiver, he should focus on the receiver's inside lower number. When the receiver's number raises up, the defender must lower his body and prepare to break on the receiver's pattern.

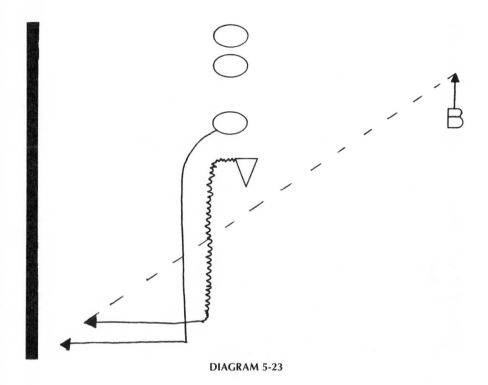

DIAGRAM 5-23

Drill #7: Trail Drill—Downfield Inside Route

Purpose: To teach defensive backs the techniques of playing man coverage underneath the receiver when executing the Two-Deep Man Under coverage.

Procedure: This drill is operated the same way as Drill #6, with the exception that the receiver will run a 10- to 15-yard inside route. (See Diagram 5-24.)

Coaching Points: The technique emphasis is similar to Drill #6 until the break of the receiver. It is important for the defender to ignore all outside moves. The defensive back's inside alignment will give him an advantage on defending the inside route. When the receiver breaks inside, the defensive back must continue to focus his eyes on the receiver until he feels he has control of the receiver's pattern.

A common problem with defending the inside break is that the defensive back looks to the quarterback on the break. If the defender makes this error, the receiver could run inside and then back outside. The receiver could also run a Post, therefore eluding the defensive back. The corner

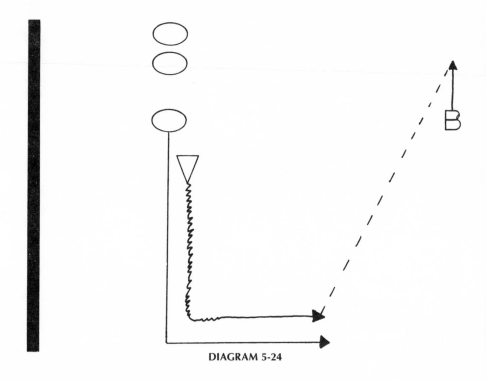

DIAGRAM 5-24

should be between the quarterback and the receiver, making it impossible for the pass to be completed.

A coach may add to this drill by intermittently quick-releasing the receiver inside. Drills #6 and #7 can be combined. The advanced phase of the Trail Drill is to have the receiver fake an inside break and run an outside break. The receiver can also fake an outside break and run an inside break.

Drill #8: Rip and Club Drill

Purpose: To teach a defensive back how to separate the football from a receiver after a pass is completed.

Procedure: Many times when a receiver and a quarterback perfectly execute an offensive play a defensive back is put in a position of either giving up a completion or dislodging the ball from the receiver for an incomplete pass. There are several methods of stripping the ball, but we have found the Rip and Club technique is the most efficient.

This drill is executed by having two lines of defensive backs, one line represents the receivers, and the other will be a line of defensive backs who will execute the Rip and Club technique.

The coach stands facing the two lines at a distance of 10 yards away. The line representing receivers will be one stride closer to the coach to symbolize having position on the defensive back. When the coach brings the ball to a throwing position, the receiver and defensive back will run at three-fourths speed toward the coach. The coach will throw the ball to the receiver and the defensive back will execute the Rip and Club technique by ripping the arms with the hand nearest the quarterback, or coach, and clubbing the helmet with the opposite arm at almost the same time.

Coaching Points: It is very important to regulate the tempo of the drill, as it can be a very aggressive drill if it is not controlled. The defender should execute the rip motion as the ball is touched by the receiver, with the club arm following slightly after contact with the ball. The complete technique must be played as though the defender is playing the football and not the receiver. It is against the rules to strike an opponent's head, so the defender must be going through the helmet to get to the football.

This maneuver will take the receiver's eyes off the football, and hopefully, will result in an incomplete pass. The defender must also work his hips between the receiver and the goal line so that he will not slip off the ball carrier and give up a big play. If the Rip and Club technique does not strip the ball, the defender will work himself into a good tackle position and get the receiver to the ground.

Drill #9: Alignment and Post Corner Drill

Purpose: To reinforce proper vertical and horizontal alignment of the defensive back.

Procedure: This is an excellent drill to run every day to ensure that the defender works hard on his backpedal and to execute a break to either a corner route or a post route, therefore emphasizing good hip and feet movement.

Begin the drill with a line of defensive backs who represent receivers. One defensive back will align six to seven yards in depth from the receiver and one imaginary man either inside or outside leverage depending on the basic coverage being worked on. Two cones are aligned on the field at a point 15 yards from the receiver line and 10 yards apart. When the receivers move, the defensive back will begin to backpedal full speed, keeping his cushion on the receiver both vertically and horizontally. The receiver will be running at three-fourths speed and trying to stem outside of the defender's lateral cushion. When the receiver gets to the cones, or 15 yards up the field, he will run either a corner route or a post route.

It is important that the receiver not run his route before 15 yards because this forces the defensive back to stay in his backpedal and not turn his body too early, which is a common fault in backpedalling.

When the defensive back breaks on the receiver's route, he then gets in good position on the upfield shoulder of the potential receiver. There is no ball used in this drill so the coach can isolate the backpedal, leverage and turn techniques. These techniques are vital when achieving and maintaining proper position on a receiver. (See Diagram 5-25.)

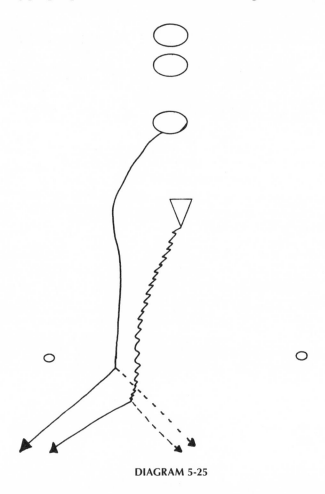

DIAGRAM 5-25

Coaching Points: Make sure the receivers run less than full speed so the defender feels comfortable in his backpedal. As the players become more experienced with the drill, the receiver can gradually increase his speed. The receiver also must execute the proper post or corner move exactly. The coach must be very specific at the aiming point he wants the receiver to break on both routes. If he is not specific, he will get a variety of angles on the routes, and the purpose of the drill will be lost.

6

Selected Techniques and Drills for Coaching the Safety to Execute Basic Coverages

Safeties must be able to perform both man and zone coverage techniques to be successful on the football field. The man technique discussed in the previous chapter on cornerback play is very similar to the technique that safeties must develop and master in order to play man-to-man coverage.

This chapter will concentrate on safety techniques utilized when playing zone technique, such as Three-Deep Zone, Man Free, Two-Deep Zone and Two-Deep Man coverages.

The safeties are the leaders, or quarterbacks, of the defensive backfield. Safeties are more centrally located on the field and, therefore, must be able to call out coverage adjustments and additional important communication to their teammates because they are in a better position to observe the offensive formation.

COMMUNICATION TECHNIQUE

It is important for all pass defenders to talk to each other when a play develops, but the safeties must be taught the importance of taking the leadership for the secondary. The safety should communicate everything he sees that will help a teammate. The importance of the defender yelling key information loud and clear to his teammates cannot be overemphasized.

Safeties should continually be calling out formations, coverage checks and cover calls before the snap of the ball. At the snap, deep backs should call out run or pass as soon as it is determined. On running plays, they should sound off on option, sweep, crack, draw, etc. On passing plays they should yell cross, in, out, hook, post, screen, ball, etc. In order to get maximum coverage from the linebackers, as well as each other, the safeties should let their teammates know what is happening. Most of the receivers are behind the intermediate and short coverage, therefore, the linebackers are unable to see what they are doing.

Points to remember in safety communication procedure:

1. Recognize the formation when the offense lines up and sound it out loud and clear, i.e., "pro right," "split left" or "pro left."
2. Immediately give coverage checks, if any, pass coverage calls and run support calls to the defensive back on his side as well as the linebackers, i.e., "check wide," "cloud," "right," etc.
3. Last-minute reminders should be given to teammates, i.e., "watch the seam," "squeeze it," "watch halfback pass," etc.
4. Read the keys to determine the run or pass and call out what is seen loud and clear.
5. On runs, be ready to communicate, i.e., "crack," "option," "sweep," "draw," etc.
6. On passes, TALK, i.e., "cross," "out," "curl," "up," "screen," etc.

READING THE QUARTERBACK TECHNIQUE

Several methods of reading the quarterback are used to get a good break on the ball. The quarterback's first steps will aid in determining where he is going to throw the football. His first steps and body lean are very important.

When the quarterback comes down the line of scrimmage the play will be a run or play-action pass. When the quarterback moves away from the line of scrimmage and leans in that direction, the play will be a drop-back or sprint-out pass.

When the offense is executing a misdirection play, the defensive back should hesitate slightly to get a look at the entire picture. A defender must get an early read on the direction of the pass. Sprint-out or half sprint-out restricts the passer's field. Through specific motions, the quarterback telegraphs his intention to the defender to that side that the throw is going to be in his direction. His motions also tell the defensive back to the opposite side that it will be an inward breaking pattern, usually of a deeper nature.

When facing a quarterback who drops back, a defender must depend on formation, motion, hash-mark position and the receiver threats. The depth of the drop will indicate if it is to be a short or long pass. Two to three steps will normally be a short pass. Six to seven steps will be a longer, or more complicated pattern.

A majority of the time the quarterback's eyes will come in contact with the receiver before he releases the football. His setup is important as related to his torso. The quarterback's shoulder and arm also furnish specific reads to the defender on the direction of the ball. The receiver in line with the quarterback's shoulder and arm will be the primary target.

The actual release of the football can be read from the quarterback's form. In order to throw the ball, the quarterback must utilize his opposite arm as a counterbalance. When this arm approaches its ready, or up, position the football will be delivered shortly thereafter. It is important to analyze the throwing habits of the opposing quarterbacks because they will all have a particular characteristic which will allow the defender to get a good break on the football.

On the drop-back, half-sprint or set actions, the quarterback will shift his weight forward at the moment before his release. This shift is a positive read that will enable the defender to begin his pursuit to the target area. These cues complement the defender's techniques and aid communication and breaking on the football. The defensive back should always be striving to find quarterback habits that will aid his jump on the football.

The defender should watch the quarterback from the time he leaves the huddle until he delivers the football. Most quarterbacks will differ in their setup and release, so defensive backs must, through video analysis, study the opposing quarterback for keys.

HASH TECHNIQUE

If a safety can develop the hash technique, he is well on his way to becoming a successful safety. This technique is used specifically by safeties when executing Two-Deep Zone and Two-Deep Man Under coverages. Corners and the free safety use the same mechanics and theory when they are playing a Three-Deep Zone coverage.

The defender must realize where his help is when executing the Hash technique. In both coverages, Two-Deep Man and Two-Deep Zone, his help is between the line of scrimmage and his initial alignment, which should be 12 to 14 yards deep. The safety should key the quarterback and get depth, using a good sound backpedal while reading the quarterback's eyes and his setup for delivery of the football. It is important to stay on the inside edge of the hash mark and ignore all receiver routes. If the defensive back is watching receivers, he cannot get a true key on the quarterback's release of the football.

When the quarterback does throw the football, the defender should break for the ball, watching it from the time it is released to the time when the defensive back either makes the interception or makes a play on the football.

Most quarterbacks will have a certain release characteristic which will allow the defensive back to get a good jump on the football. It is important to study a quarterback's idiosyncrasies so the safety will have a definite advantage when breaking to the football. All quarterbacks will tend to watch their primary receiver, especially if sufficient pressure is applied with a good pass rush.

FREE SAFETY GETTING ONTO THE FIELD TECHNIQUE

Many times it is strategically beneficial for a free safety to show an alignment that he uses when in one coverage and run into, or stem to, another alignment and be in the called coverage. This alignment strategy is called disguising coverages. An example of executing a disguised coverage would be for the defender to line up on the hash mark, thus giving the impression that he is in a Two-Deep alignment, and then at the snap of the ball turning and running to the middle of the field while actually being in a centerfield type of coverage. (See Diagram 6-1.)

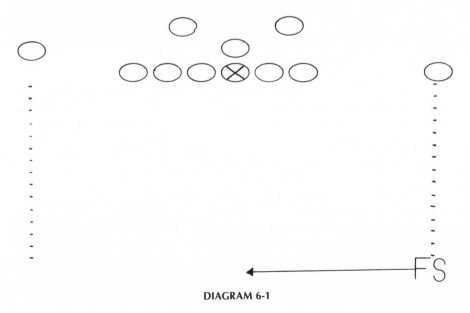

DIAGRAM 6-1

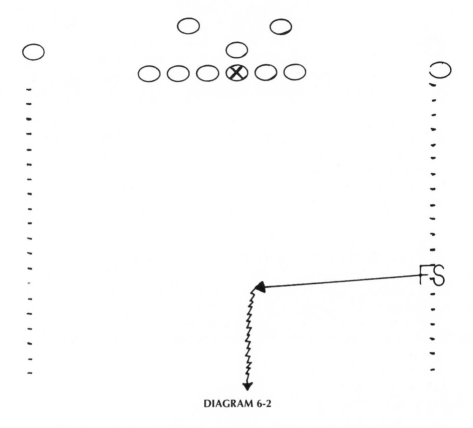

DIAGRAM 6-2

When getting onto the field and maintaining a centerfield alignment, it is important for the defender to run to the middle of the field to get maximum depth and then get into his backpedal and focus his eyes on the quarterback. (See Diagram 6-2.)

The basic coverages which utilize the Getting Onto the Field technique are Man Free and Three-Deep Zone. Safeties can also align to look as if they are in Blitz coverage and run onto the field actually being in a centerfield or free alignment.

CENTERFIELD TECHNIQUE

The free safety must be well versed in playing the Centerfield technique in both Man Free and Three-Deep Zone coverages. His alignment is 12 to 14 yards deep in the middle of the field. This technique is very similar to the Hash technique but, of course, the alignment on the football field is different.

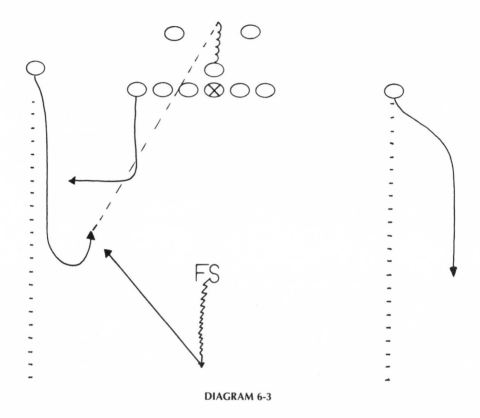

DIAGRAM 6-3

The defensive back must work hard in his backpedal getting good depth while keying the quarterback. He should not look at receiver routes, but should concentrate on the quarterback's release of the football, which will give him a good break on the ball. (See Diagram 6-3.)

COLLISION THE POST TECHNIQUE

When the defender is playing a coverage that utilizes playing the centerfield position, he must take pride that receivers will not want to invade his territory.

As the defender breaks on the football, he will take a direct line to any attacking Post pattern. If he gets to the ball before the receiver, he will intercept the football. If the defensive back gets to the ball at the same time as the receiver, he will collision the Post pattern and hopefully discourage the receiver from catching any more passes in the middle of the field. (See Diagram 6-4.)

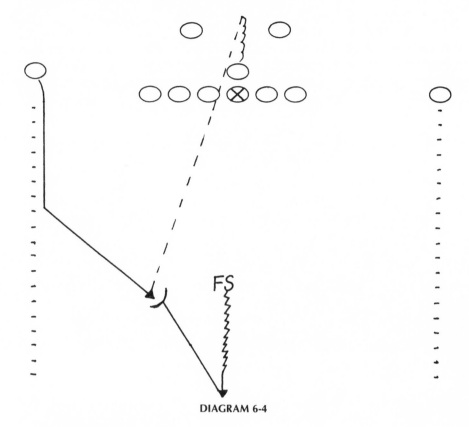

DIAGRAM 6-4

TECHNIQUE DRILLS

Drill #1: Hash Drill

Purpose: To teach the defensive back proper alignment, depth and break on the football when executing a coverage in which he is defending the deep one-half zone. Basic coverages such as Two-Deep Man and Two-Deep Zone require the defensive back to utilize this technique.

Procedure: The defensive back aligns on a hash mark at a depth of 12 to 14 yards from the line of scrimmage. A quarterback will set up at the line of scrimmage at various points between the opposite hash mark and the hash mark that the defender is on. The quarterback will take a full five- to seven-step drop. As the quarterback starts his pass drop, the defender will get into his backpedal and key the quarterback's setup. The quarterback will look in the direction that he is going to throw and he is allowed to throw the ball in the area between the middle of the goal post and the sideline.

The defender will break on the football as it leaves the quarterback's hand and intercept the ball at its highest point. When the defensive back intercepts the ball, he will run the ball back to the coach. (See Diagram 6-5.)

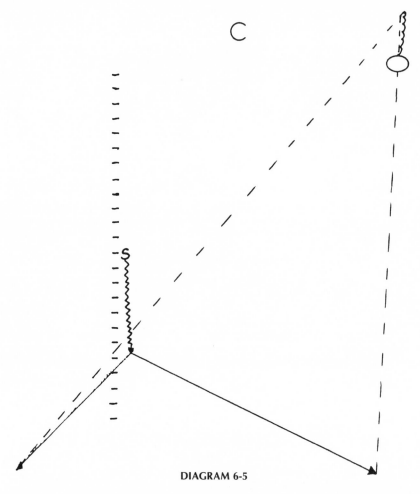

DIAGRAM 6-5

Coaching Points: For the Hash Drill to be successful, real quarterbacks must be utilized in the drill to give a proper look to the defender. It is important to emphasize to the defender that he must attack the ball at its highest point when making the interception. The defensive back must watch the ball from the point when it leaves the quarterback's hand to the time that he makes the interception.

Receivers are not used in this drill to emphasize the importance of not watching receivers, but rather of keeping the eyes on the quarterback and the football throughout the pass play to maximize the technique of getting a good break on the football. It is very important for the defensive back to work hard in his backpedal to get maximum depth so he can get a good break on the football.

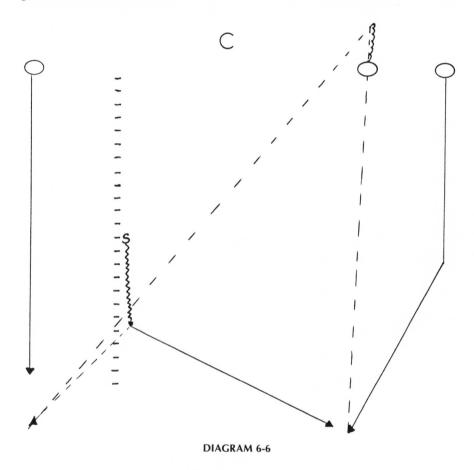

DIAGRAM 6-6

Drill #2: Hash Drill with Receivers

Purpose: To teach the defender to align, break and react to the football when playing a one-half field deep zone coverage with the pressure of having receivers running in his zone.

Procedure: The procedure of this drill is exactly the same as the Hash Drill, with the exception that two receivers are running up the field. There is one receiver on the boundary and one receiver right down the middle of the field. The defensive back gets depth, reads the quarterback and breaks on the ball. (See Diagram 6-6.)

Coaching Points: The defender must key the quarterback and not peek at the receivers running in his zone. When the ball leaves the quarterback's hand, the defensive back thinks that the ball is being thrown to him and watches it through its flight in the air until he intercepts the football.

Drill #3: Centerfield Drill

Purpose: To teach the free safety proper alignment and technique when playing deep one-third responsibilities when executing Man Free and Three-Deep Zone coverages.

Procedure: The same procedure is utilized as in the Hash Drill, with the exception that the quarterback is aligned at 12 to 14 yards deep in the middle of the field. The quarterback uses the same procedure as he did in the Hash Drill, but can align anywhere between the two hash marks. (See Diagram 6-7.)

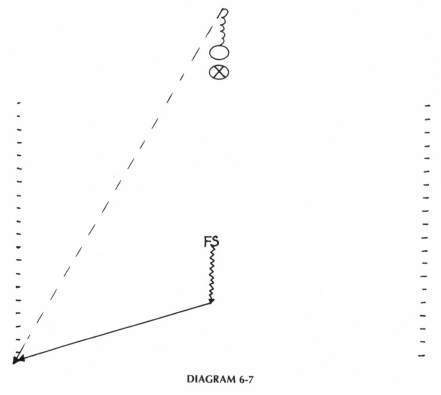

DIAGRAM 6-7

Coaching Points: Receivers can be added to this drill, but the defender must be coached to keep his eyes on the quarterback until the ball is released, thus allowing him to get a good break on the football.

7

Theories and Design
of Secondary Play

As one discusses the techniques, drills, coverages and other considerations of coaching the defensive backfield, one must also investigate the theory behind these football fundamentals. Factors such as zones of the field, formation strength, types of pass routes, as well as field position and down and distance all must be considered when developing a coverage package to attack your opponent.

ZONES OF THE FIELD

Field area awareness is important to understand when analyzing how your opponent is attacking you. Diagram 7-1 defines the areas of the field that must be defended. Strategically one must be aware of what field area the offense's game plan is attacking and be able to adjust the coverages as the game progresses.

As illustrated, the corner area designates the deep outside, or the corner of the field. The post area designates the deep middle zone that runs all the way to the goal line. Strong or weak post designates the side of the post area according to the offensive formation. Short post is an area 10 to 12 yards deep from the fan area to the post and just behind the slot area.

The flat is an outside short zone from the line of scrimmage back to a depth of approximately 10 yards. The slot area goes from the line of scrimmage back to a depth of approximately 12 yards and between the outside receiver and strongside tight end, and on the weakside between the wide receiver and weak tackle.

The hook area extends over the tight ends to a depth of approximately 15 yards. The middle area runs from the line of scrimmage to a depth of

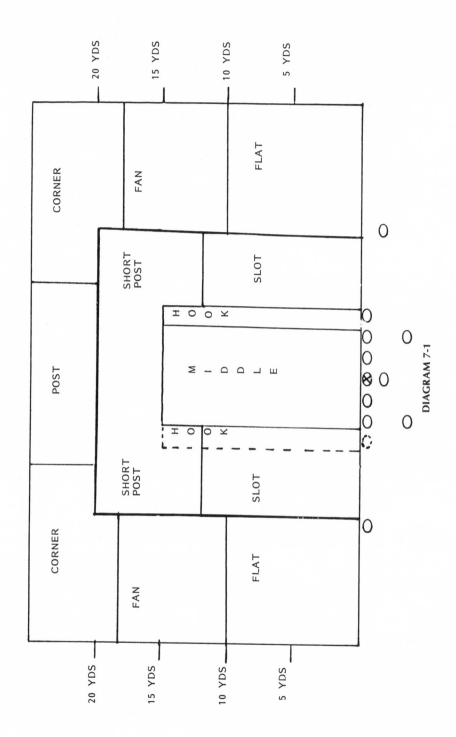

DIAGRAM 7-1

approximately 15 yards and from tackle to tackle. The fan area consists of the middle outside area between the flat and corner 15 to 18 yards in depth.

Down and distance is also a factor when defending the field, as well as actual field position. Many offensive teams will have glaring tendencies, but one must be able to make game-time adjustments according to the offensive attack.

FORMATION STRENGTH

Formation strength must be recognized quickly and accurately. There are different theories on determination of strength. The simplest method of recognizing the strength of an offensive formation for the running game is to use the position of the tight end, as Diagram 7-2 illustrates.

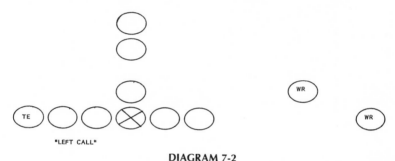

DIAGRAM 7-2

All of the alignments and adjustments, as far as the line and linebackers are concerned, will be made to the tight end.

Strength of the passing game is determined by the position of two of the offense's normal receivers, as is shown in Diagram 7-3.

Normal receivers of an offense are considered to be the two wide receivers and the tight end. If one of the backs in Diagram 7-3 was to flank on either side of the formation, the strength for run and pass would not

DIAGRAM 7-3

change. If a third wide receiver was to be substituted for a back the strength rules would hold true. If the set was balanced as in Diagrams 7-4 or 7-5, a determination of strength would have to be made by personnel, hash alignment or some reason determined within your game plan for your opponent.

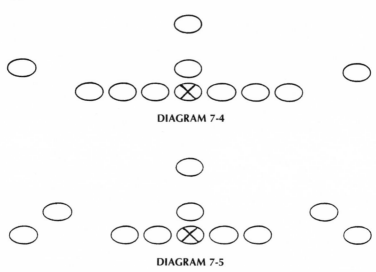

DIAGRAM 7-4

DIAGRAM 7-5

Motion

Motion will not affect the strength rules. Strength may change because of motion, but the tight end remains strength for run and the two receivers will remain strength for the pass. Diagram 7-6 illustrates that motion changes the strength of the formation but the strength rules stay constant.

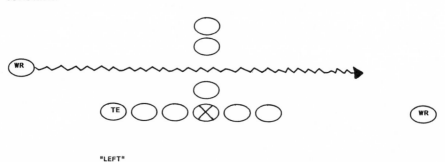

"LEFT"

PASS STRENGTH WOULD BE A "LOUIE" ORIGINALLY, THE MOTION WOULD CHECK TO "ROGER"

DIAGRAM 7-6

Backfield motion will not affect run and pass strength. Slight adjustments may be needed to stretch zones and linebacker drops but the run/pass strength remains constant.

Multiple Sets

Strength of multiple sets not utilizing a tight end should be determined by the two wide receivers. If the multiple set is balanced, a strength determination must be predetermined.

The entire team should have full knowledge of formation strengths as well as formation recognition. The defensive backfield in particular must be able to recognize formations to make any game-plan adjustment according to tendencies. Formations which are most commonly used are illustrated in Diagrams 7-7 through 7-14.

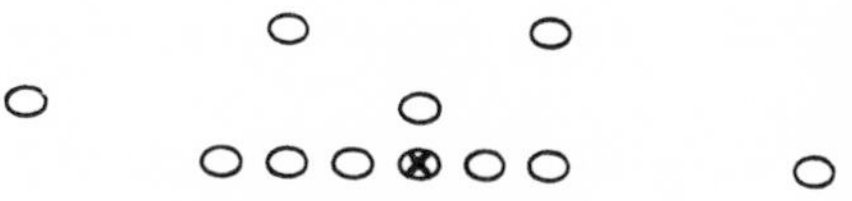

DIAGRAM 7-7

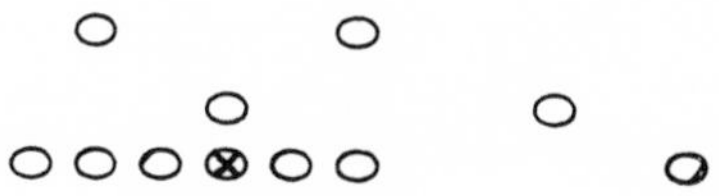

DIAGRAM 7-8

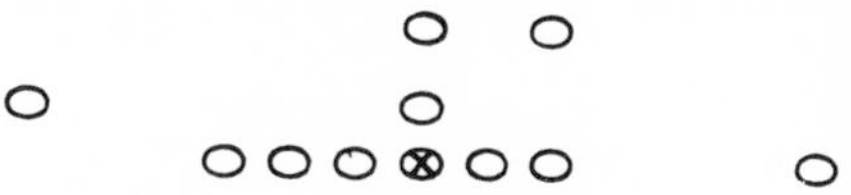

DIAGRAM 7-9

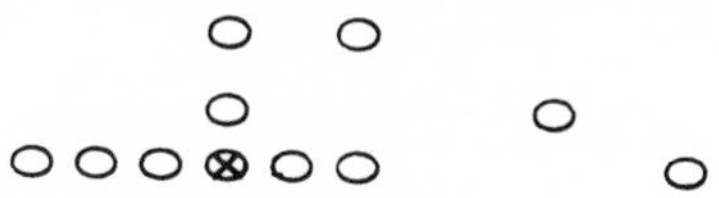

DIAGRAM 7-10

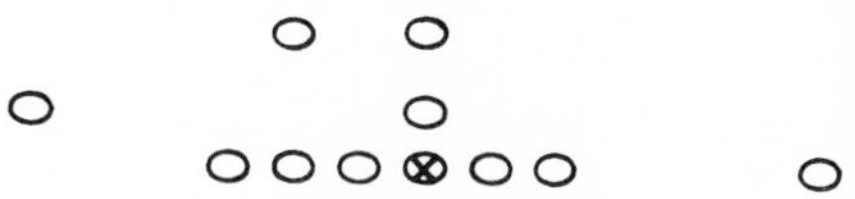

DIAGRAM 7-11

DIAGRAM 7-12

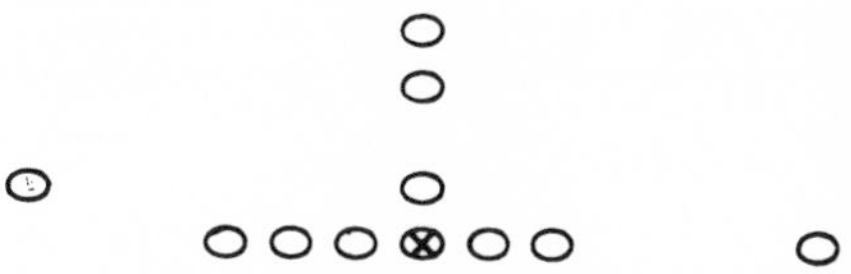

DIAGRAM 7-13

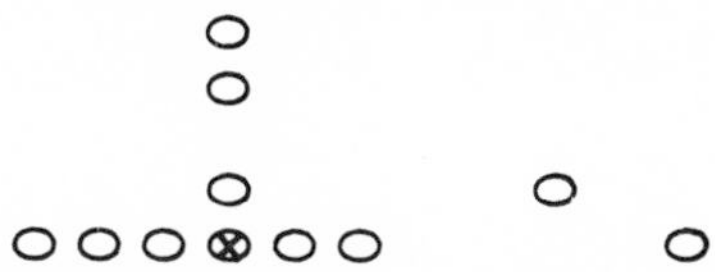

DIAGRAM 7-14

Irregular Personnel

Formations utilizing irregular personnel are illustrated in Diagrams 7-15 through 7-19. The Ace formation utilizes two tight ends, two wide receivers and one running back. The Jacks formation employs three tight ends and two running backs. The Kings formation utilizes three wide receivers, one tight end and one running back. The Queens formation has three wide receivers and two running backs. In the Flush formation there are four wide receivers and one running back.

IRREGULAR PERSONNEL

ACE

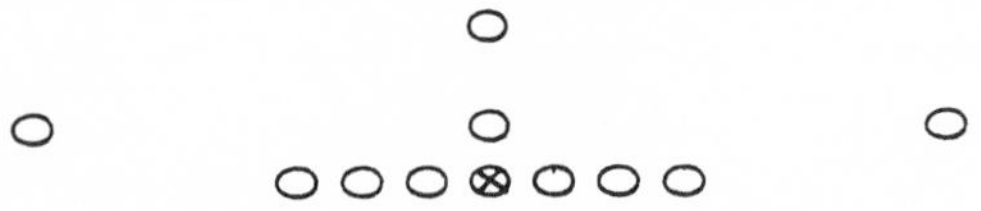

DIAGRAM 7-15

JACKS

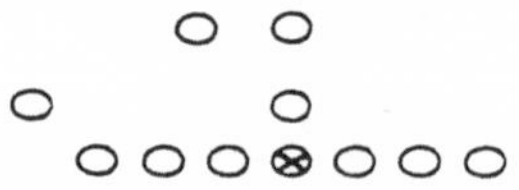

DIAGRAM 7-16

KINGS

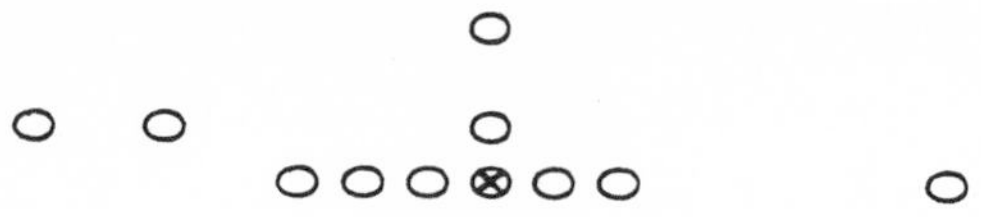

DIAGRAM 7-17

QUEENS

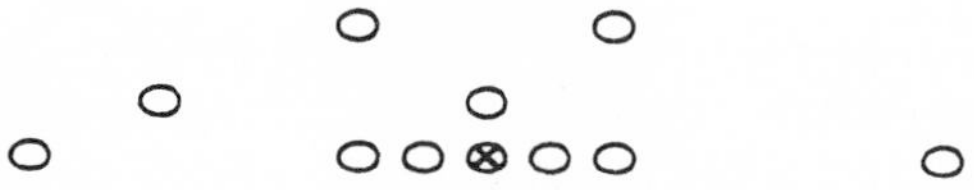

DIAGRAM 7-18

FLUSH

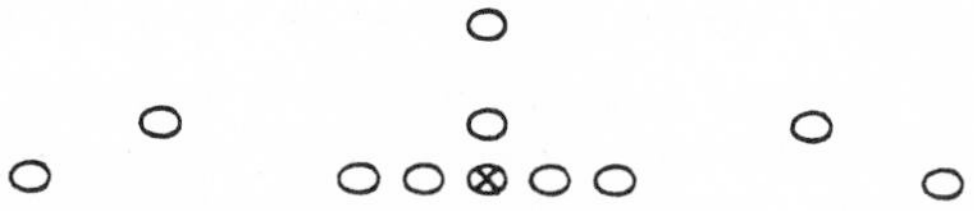

DIAGRAM 7-19

RECEIVER ROUTES

The defensive back must be familiar with the knowledge and terminology of receiver routes. The basic term for a route may vary from coach to coach, but there are fundamental routes which must be understood by the defensive backfield.

Individual Running Back Pass Routes and Techniques

Diagram 7-20 on page 84 illustrates the following running back pass routes:

On the Flare route, the receiver drives to the outside with a slight belly. After driving five yards, he looks back for the ball, continuing on the route.

When executing the Short Fan, the receiver drives at the outside shoulder of the linebacker to a point two to three yards downfield. He then breaks parallel to the line of scrimmage at full speed looking for the ball over his outside shoulder on the break.

Positive movement at the linebacker is taken during the Circle route. The receiver continues upfield, looking for the ball immediately after crossing the line of scrimmage.

The receiver drives at the outside shoulder of the linebacker, continuing upfield full speed six yards when performing the Fan route. He breaks toward the sideline at a 90-degree angle looking for the ball over his outside shoulder.

Diagram 7-21 on page 85 illustrates the following running back pass routes:

On the Sky route a receiver starts directly toward a point three yards outside the outside linebacker. He heads upfield looking for the ball over his inside shoulder upon crossing the line of scrimmage.

When running the Angle route the receiver drives to a point four yards outside the linebacker, continuing upfield to a point where he can cut back inside the linebacker covering him. When he cuts back, he drives hard to the inside, almost parallel to the line of scrimmage, looking for the ball on the break.

On the Flag or Corner route he runs a "circle" and at a point eight to ten yards downfield drives to the outside at a 45-degree angle, looking for the ball over the outside shoulder on the break.

The receiver runs a Short Fan looking back at the quarterback to pull the defensive man up on him, driving full speed downfield, looking for the ball over the inside shoulder when executing the Shoot and Up.

Diagram 7-22 on page 86 illustrates the following running back pass routes:

On the Check Down route the back emulates pass protections. He delays three counts, then drives straight downfield between the offensive guard and the tackle looking for the ball immediately after clearing the

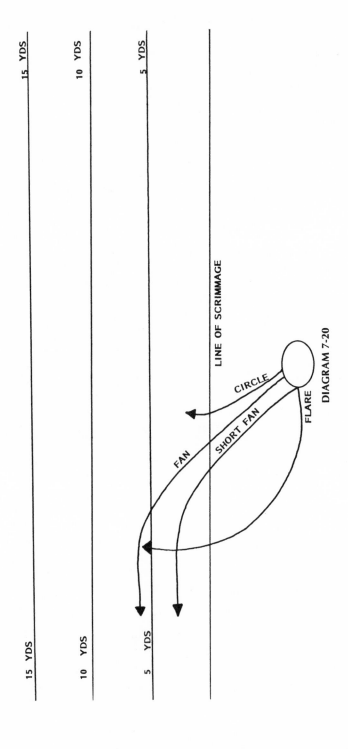

DIAGRAM 7-20

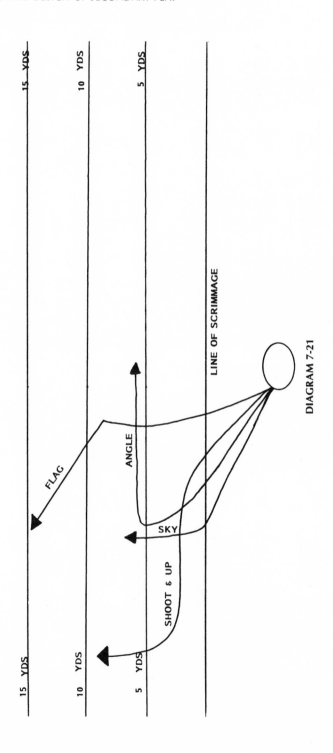

DIAGRAM 7-21

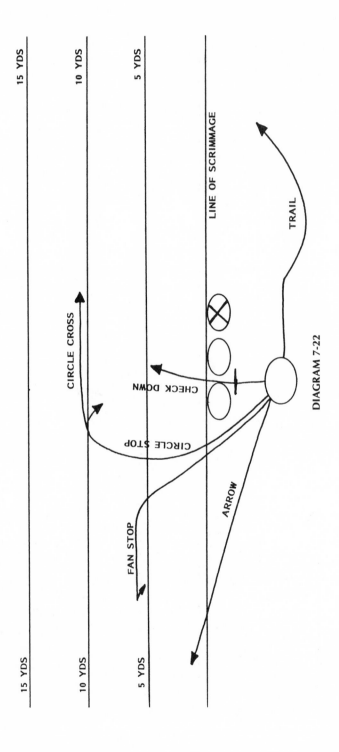

DIAGRAM 7-22

line of scrimmage. He is always alert as to the position of the linebacker to the side of delay.

The back runs a "circle" then continues upfield about 10 yards and curls to the inside when running the Circle Stop.

When running the Circle Cross route the back runs a "circle" continuing downfield about 10 yards, then drives inside almost parallel to the line of scrimmage looking for the ball over the inside shoulder on the break.

On the Fan Stop route the back runs a "fan." When the linebacker is running with him, he stops, plants his outside foot and looks for the ball. He is always alert for the position of the linebacker.

The Trail route starts parallel to the line of scrimmage toward the remaining back. Upon reaching the fullback position the receiver begins running a Flare pattern.

When running the Arrow route the receiver sprints to a spot well outside the linebacker. He runs almost parallel to the line of scrimmage, gaining ground only slightly. He looks for the ball on the third step.

Individual Wide Receiver Pass Routes

Diagram 7-23 on page 88 illustrates the following wide receiver pass routes:

The Fast Hitch route is executed by the receiver taking one hard step downfield, then shuffling back. He gets his head around quickly. The ball will be thrown on his back side hip.

On the Hitch the receiver explodes off the line, running at the defensive man for three or four steps. He plants his outside foot, turning to the quarterback. If the ball is not thrown immediately, he pivots to the outside and runs an "up."

The Slant pattern is run by the receiver exploding off the line, running at the defensive man for two or three steps. He drives off his outside foot to the inside at a 30-degree angle. He looks for the ball on the first step after he breaks.

When executing the Quick Post the receiver explodes off the line and runs downfield for five yards. He drives off his outside foot at a 30-degree angle to the inside. He looks for the ball on his first step after the break.

The China route is an underneath route where the receiver starts downfield for one step, comes under control and delays until the pattern develops, then he runs a "slant." He looks for the ball on his first step after the break.

Diagram 7-24 on page 89 illustrates the following wide receiver pass routes:

On a Short Out the receiver runs at the defensive man for five yards. He drives off the inside foot at a 90-degree angle to the outside. He looks for the ball on his first step after the break.

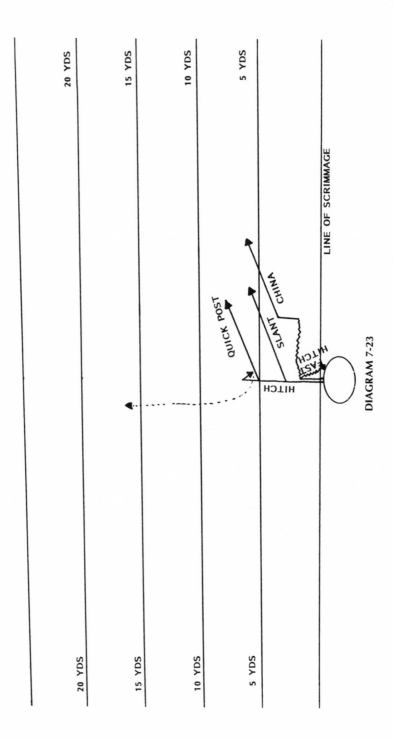

DIAGRAM 7-23

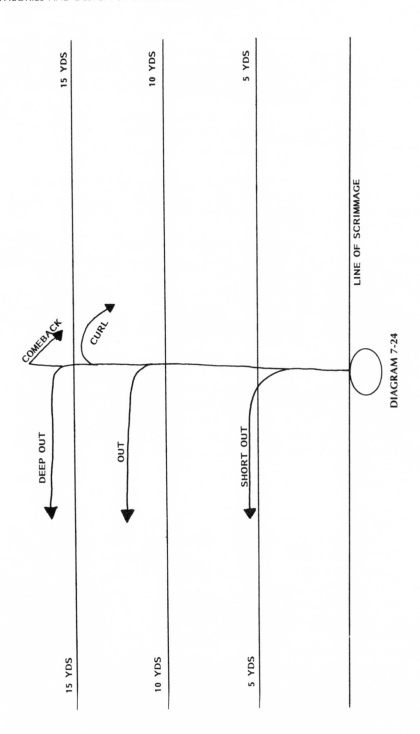

DIAGRAM 7-24

The Out is run at the defensive man for 10 to 12 yards. The receiver drives off his inside foot and breaks at a 90-degree angle to the outside. He looks for the ball on his first step after the break.

The Deep Out is run at the defensive man for 14 to 16 yards. He drives off his inside foot and the sideline and comes back at a 45-degree angle. He keeps coming back until the catch is made.

The receiver runs at the defensive man for 10 to 12 yards, driving off his outside foot to the inside at a 90-degree angle when running an In route.

The Curl route is run at the defensive man for 12 to 14 yards. The receiver circles to his inside, finding an open spot between the linebackers. He will come back to the ball until the catch has been made.

The Comeback, or Stop, is run at the defensive man for 14 to 16 yards. The receiver drives off his outside foot to the inside, coming back at a 45-degree angle. He gets his head around quickly. He comes back to meet the ball until the catch is made.

Diagram 7-25 on page 91 illustrates the following wide receiver pass routes:

The Corner route is run at the defensive man for five yards. The receiver drives to the inside as if running a Deep Slant for three steps then drives off his inside foot to the corner.

The Post is run at the defensive man for eight yards. The receiver drives off his outside foot at a 30-degree angle to the inside.

When executing the Up route the receiver runs at the defensive man for six to seven yards. He accelerates past the defensive man fading slightly to the outside. He makes the catch over his inside shoulder.

The Flag route is run at the defensive man for eight to twelve yards. The receiver drives off his inside foot to the flag, or the corner, of the end zone.

Individual Tight End Pass Patterns

Diagram 7-26 on page 92 illustrates the following tight end pass patterns:

On the Lookie route the tight end releases inside the linebacker and straightens up as soon as possible and looks for the ball quickly. He catches the ball over his inside shoulder.

The Diagonal route has the tight end release into the linebacker, driving him off the line of scrimmage. He releases quickly to the outside at a 30-degree angle. He looks for the ball on his first step after releasing from the linebacker.

When executing the Over route the tight end releases inside of the linebacker. After releasing the linebacker, he angles to the weakside at a 30-degree angle. He looks for the ball after clearing the linebacker. He continues to run if the ball is not thrown.

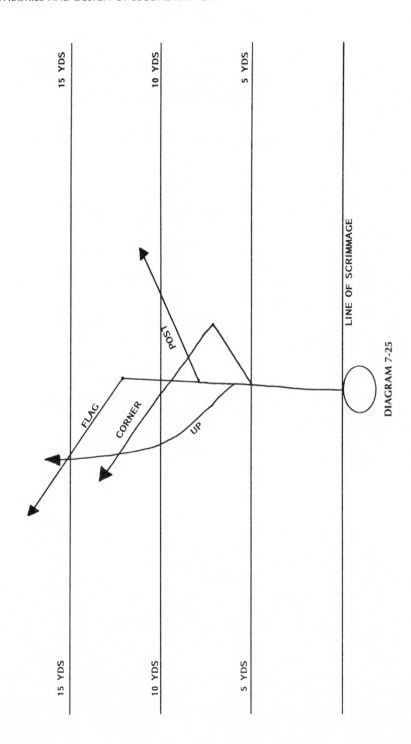

DIAGRAM 7-25

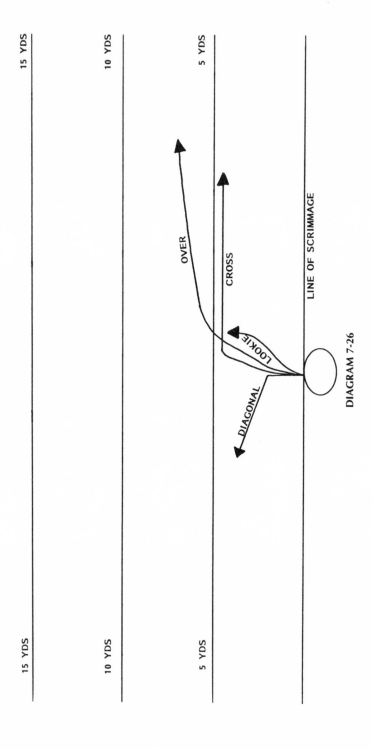

DIAGRAM 7-26

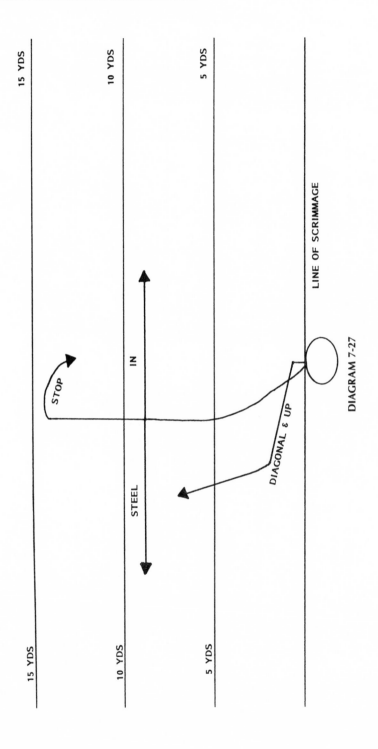

DIAGRAM 7-27

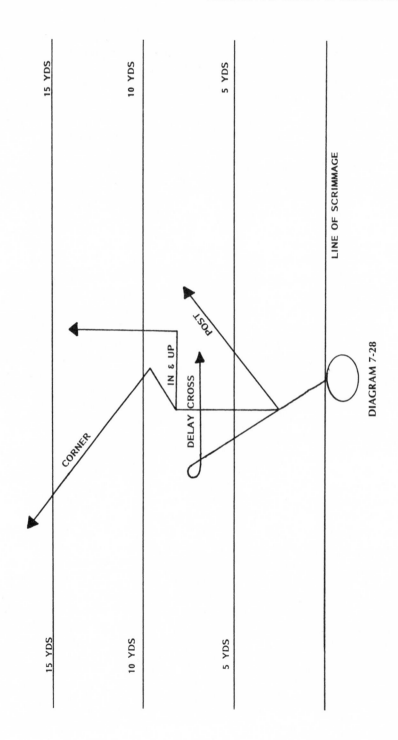

DIAGRAM 7-28

The Cross route release is inside of the linebacker. He runs upfield for four to five yards, drives off his outside foot to the inside, almost parallel to the line of scrimmage. He looks for the ball on the first step after the break.

Diagram 7-27 on page 93 illustrates the following tight end pass routes:

The In route release is outside of the linebacker. The receiver runs at the defensive man for eight to ten yards and drives off the outside foot to the inside at a 90-degree angle.

When running the Stop route, the release is outside of the linebacker. The tight end runs at the defensive man for 12 to 14 yards. He circles to the inside finding the open spot between the linebackers. He gets his head around quickly and comes back until the catch is made.

The Steel route release is outside of the linebacker. The receiver runs at the defensive man for eight to ten yards. He drives off his inside foot to the outside at a 90-degree angle.

The Diagonal and Up is started by running a Straight route for three to five steps and then turning "up" and sprinting upfield.

Diagram 7-28 on page 94 illustrates the following tight end pass routes:

The Corner route release is outside of the linebacker and run at the defensive man for eight to ten yards. The receiver drives off the outside foot to the inside for three steps as if to run a "stop." Then he drives off his inside foot to the corner. He looks for the ball on his first step after the break, but the distance may vary.

When executing the Post pattern, the release is outside of the linebacker as if running a Straight until the backer commits, then he breaks sharply back to the inside.

The In and Up pattern release is outside of the linebacker. The tight end runs at the defensive man eight to ten yards. He drives off the outside foot to the inside at a 90-degree angle for two to three steps and then drives off his inside foot and runs an Up route. The ball will be caught over the inside shoulder.

The Delay Cross route release is outside of the linebacker. The receiver works outside, then pivots or delays, allowing the back to clear. Then he comes back across the formation looking for the ball as he breaks clear.

When discussing formations, strength, pass routes or other football terminology it is important to utilize one-word terms whenever possible for ease in communication and learning. It is important to simplify the terms to allow the player to concentrate on reaction, movement, pursuit and tackling. It is advantageous to eliminate anything that takes away from an athlete's ability to play football.

8

Theories of Coverage

The first considerations in establishing a pass coverage philosophy, or stopping a team in a particular passing situation, are whether to rush or cover, whether to use man, zone or combination coverage, or whether to defend field or formation.

We will analyze the most common coverages which are in the three categories of man, zone or combo coverage. From the zone group we will discuss Three-Deep Zone and Two-Deep Zone. Combination coverages selected will be Two-Deep Zone Man Underneath and Three-Deep Weak Roll. Man coverages will include Reading Man-to-Man, Man with a Free Safety and Dog or Blitz Man.

There are many more coverages that are used, but these coverages are the most extensively used and parts of these coverages, techniques and theories are used in all other possible combinations of coverages.

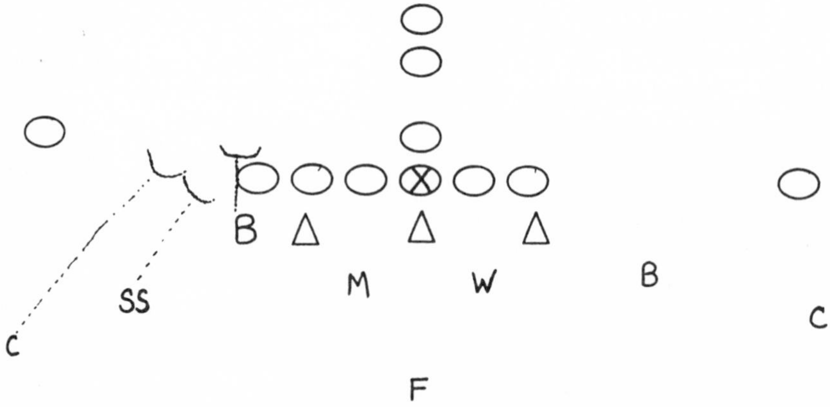

DIAGRAM 8-1

RUN SUPPORT

A defensive back's most important task is defending the pass, but it is also vitally important that he execute his run support role. The secondary is responsible not only for any long pass, but also for any long run. To be the primary run support they must contain the play. If the ball carrier breaks the perimeter, it is the responsibility of the secondary support man to make the game-saving open-field tackle.

In the study of the selected coverages run support will be discussed as Safety Force, Corner Force or Backer Force.

Strongside Forces

Strongside force includes safety, corner and backer force to the two-receiver side, as illustrated in Diagram 8-1.

Safety Force: When the safety has primary outside force, his key is the tight end. He should start his force as the tight end blocks. His ability to see the flow as well as the pulling linemen will ensure quick force of the play. When the tight end blocks or hook blocks, the safety should meet the lead blocker as fast as possible, never deeper than one yard in the backfield. He should turn the play inside, yet be in position to react back to the inside. He should never give himself up one for one on the lead blocker.

The strong backer has the cutback area. If the tight end blocks down, the strong backer takes position to play the cutback. He should control the blocker who attacks him, not taking a side, and get to the football and make the play. If the tight end blocks the strong backer, he should control him from outside-in, leverage him to the inside, and disengage.

The strong corner is the secondary force. He should play pass until the flanker either blocks him or crack-back blocks to the inside. It is important that he play pass until his key of the flanker definitely tells him it is run. If the flanker cracks on inside support, the strong corner then takes the responsibility of primary force and must contain the play.

Diagram 8-2 illustrates both the safety force and the strong corner force.

Strong Corner Force: When the strong corner is the primary outside force his key should be inside through the backfield to the quarterback. If the flow comes to him he must turn the play inside by meeting the lead blocker in or behind the line of scrimmage as fast as possible, turn the play to the inside, yet be in position to react back to the outside. If the lead blocker is well out in front of the ball carrier he may elude the blocker to get to the ball, but must never give up his outside arm or leg, which would cause a loss of containment. The corner should also never give himself up one for one with the lead blocker and never penetrate more than one yard into the backfield.

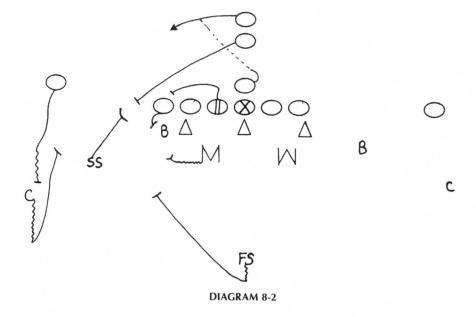

DIAGRAM 8-2

If the corner is blocked by the receiver, he must elude the block, squeeze down the field area and contain the football.

The strong backer has the cutback area just as he does with safety support. The safety has secondary force and will play pass until the outside receiver blocks.

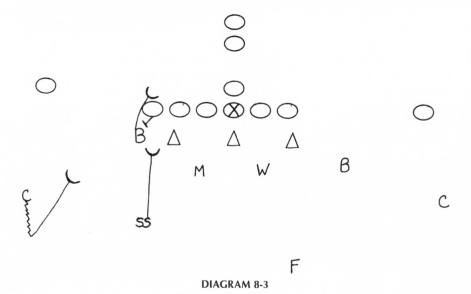

DIAGRAM 8-3

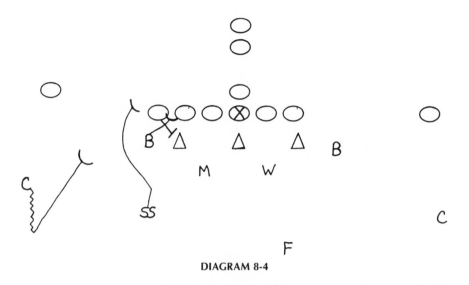

DIAGRAM 8-4

Backer Force: If the tight end releases or blocks on the strong backer, he is the primary outside force. He should control the tight end from outside in and contain the play, as Diagram 8-3 illustrates.

The safety has the cutback area and will fill inside at the ball. The strong corner is secondary force and will not be involved in the play unless his receiver gives him a run key.

Backer force will change to a read force or safety force if the tight end blocks down. When the tight end blocks down, the strong backer will take the cutback area. The safety will become the primary outside force with the corner becoming the secondary force, as is illustrated in Diagram 8-4.

When the corner, safety or backer has primary force, he should always be in a position to effectively force and make the tackle. He needs to get outside position, but not get so wide or so far upfield that the force is wasted. He must fight to keep the hole as small as possible, therefore allowing the cutback man to be an effective tackler. He should always keep his outside arm free, and his outside leg back and free. This will allow him to make the play or bounce the ball. As a cutback man, he should make the tackle with good force; the hole should be narrow enough that he can make an effective tackle. He should never overrun the force man. The angle will vary slightly with difference in force.

9

Coaching the Defensive Back on Game Day

A defensive back can be fundamentally and strategically sound, but if he is not mentally prepared for competition he may not play the game to his full potential.

The defensive back's mental preparation begins during the first practice sessions during the week before the upcoming ball game. The coach must realistically and truthfully prepare the defenders on what they have to do physically, strategically and mentally to win the ball game.

PRACTICE

Throughout the week defensive backs must work on individual fundamentals and techniques. Defensive backs should get as much one-on-one work with receivers as possible to improve their technique. The secondary must have proper time allowed for seven-on-seven passing drills featuring their opponent's pass routes against the coverages the coach has selected to utilize. A team period featuring the opponent's runs and play-action passes should also be a part of practice. The team period should feature outside running plays to allow the defensive backs to work on their run support. A sample practice plan is illustrated in Diagram 9-1 on pages 102–103.

ASSIGNMENTS

It is important for the defensive backs to watch video on the upcoming opponent. The coach should give the players direction as to what they should be looking for.

Each defensive back should be given a particular assignment on the opponent to watch and examine during the week. The day before the game, each defensive back reports his findings to the rest of the secondary. This is an excellent way to encourage watching the next opponent, and the other players enjoy hearing from their teammates on points that will help everyone do their responsibilities better.

An example of an assignment is for a free safety to analyze the opposing quarterback's throwing action. He should look for specific habits or keys such as:

1. Does he look at the point he is going to throw to, thereby telegraphing the intended receiver?
2. Does he pat the ball before he releases it?
3. Does he scramble when his primary receiver is covered?

Anything that can be reported to the defensive backs on the quarterback's throwing characteristics is very helpful. Many times it shows the rest of the secondary how prepared and serious the reporting defender is, which is very positive for the attitude of his teammates.

TESTS

The day before the game a test should be administered to the defensive backs covering their knowledge of what has been taught during the week. The test should consist of information given to the defensive backs from the scouting report on their opponent, strategy to be utilized and any checks that might be needed at game time. A sample backfield test is presented in Diagram 9-2, beginning on page 104.

PREGAME

It is recommended that the players arrive at the stadium two hours before game time. The defensive backs should be dressed and on the field one hour before the game. Pregame should consist of a warm-up period to stride and stretch. The warm-up period should be followed by footwork drills, ball drills and tackling drills. When the rest of the team comes out, this procedure should be repeated along with full team repetitions of eleven-on-eleven, offense versus defense, before going back into the locker room to prepare for the start of the game.

UTAH PRACTICE PLAN   UTAH STATE   DATE: Tues. 8/27

PER.	TIME	SEC.	ILB	DL	OL	Y	WR/SLOT	QB	BACKS
1		UTE PURSUIT							
2		LINES M-DRILL	AGILES SLEDS	BAGS CONES					
3		TACKLING SWIM	TACKLING	CHUTES REACTION					
4		→	RUN KEYS	TACKLE KEYS					
5			TEAM OPTION						
6									
7		1 ON 1	BULL →	RUN →					
8		VS WR							
9		→	→	→					
10			WATER BREAK						
11			SPECIAL TEAMS						
12									
13									

	14	15	16	17	18	19	20	21	22	23	24	25	26
S K E L E T O N		SWIM POW (UP)	POST POW (UP)	FIELDER (UP)									
							T E A M	BLITZ (12 SNAPS)	PUP				
BASE	REACH	COUNTERS	1 ON 1	TWISTS	→								

DIAGRAM 9-1

DIAGRAM 9-2

DEFENSIVE BACKFIELD TEST VS. OREGON

1. Give an overview of Oregon, including players and offensive strategy.

2. What will Oregon try to feature offensively?

3. What was Oregon's record?

4. Evaluate and name Oregon's receiver core and QB. Also give receiver route tendencies.

5. What is Oregon's favorite running formation and what are their favorite running plays?

DIAGRAM 9-2 (cont'd)

6. What are Oregon's favorite pass sets, and draw their favorite patterns.

7. Draw and explain all secondary responsibilities when we are in Goal Line.

GOAL LINE	SS	$	FS	CAT CORNER	COVER CORNER
G/L PHYSCO					
G/L DBL ATT					
G/L SLANT					
VS FLANKER MOTION					

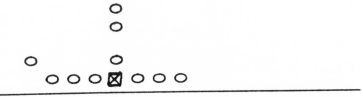

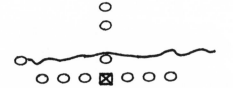

DIAGRAM 9-2 (cont'd)

8.

RESPONSIBILITIES

FORMATIONS	COVERAGES	SS	FS	$	STRONG SIDE CORNER	WEAK SIDE CORNER
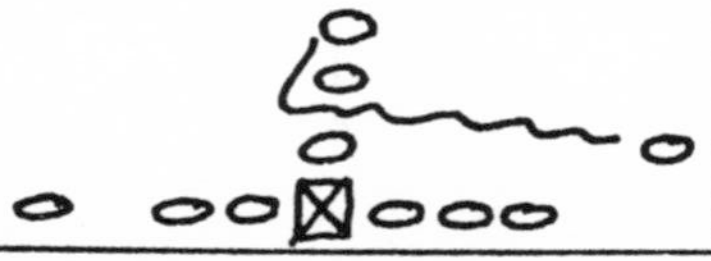	SAM ZONE					
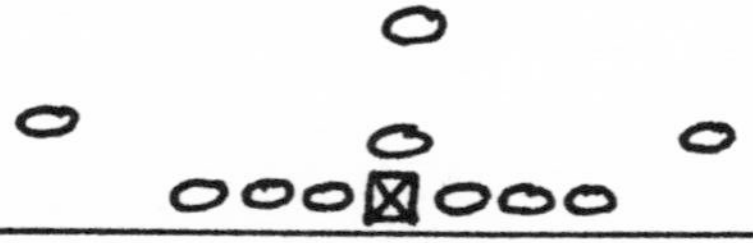	SAM ZONE DEUCE					
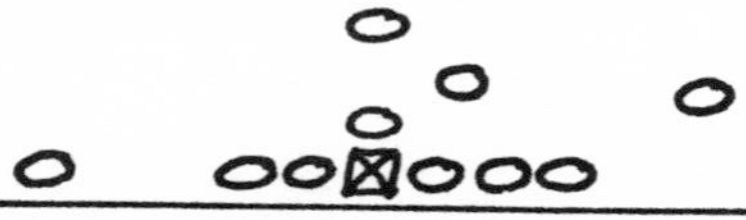	STEM/ WEED					
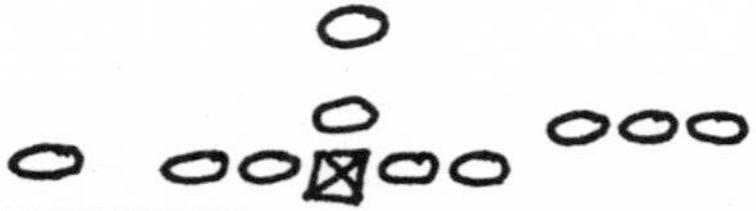	MINNESOTA					
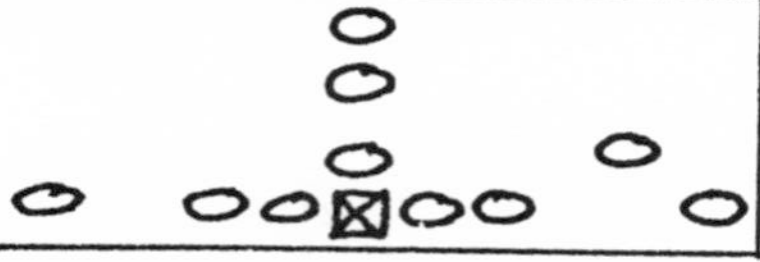	FIELDER					

SWIM/
SWIM

MINNESOTA
POST/POW

SHOW/
FIELDER

GAME TIME

During the game it is important to watch the defensive backs to make sure they are properly performing their responsibilities. Many coaches will change their game plan during a game because an opponent is moving the football, when in fact, their success is a result of a player not performing his responsibilities. A coach must direct the defender to carry out his assignment. If he physically cannot succeed, the coach should now make a strategic change to slow down the opponent.

The coaches in the press box should keep charts that will aid in determining where the opponent is trying to attack the defense. Formation hit charts, coverage hit charts, down and distance and hash charts will all help the coach and player see how the opponent is attacking their team. Samples of these charts are presented in Diagram 9-3.

It is very helpful for the coach to be able to see what is happening to his defensive backs through their eyes. This will allow for good communication.

One of the most important factors in coaching defensive backs at game time is to be positive and continually build confidence.

If the defender gets beat, the coach's job is to encourage him and reinforce the belief that the defender will make the play the next time he has the opportunity. A good defensive back can never be afraid of getting beat by an opponent; he must be fearless and confident. There are very few defensive backs in the world who have never been beaten by an opposing player sometime in their career.

Coaching the defensive back is one of the most challenging aspects involved in coaching a football team. Properly identifying the skill necessary for an athlete to play the defensive back position, precise coaching of proper technique and thorough preparation which instills confidence will create an exciting and successful defensive backfield capable of making an impact on the total team effort.

DIAGRAM 9-3

UNIVERSITY OF UTAH GAME SCRIPT   VS: _____

QTR # ___ Play No:	D &˙D	VFP	HASH	DEFENSE	OFFENSIVE PL	RESULT

DIAGRAM 9-3 (cont'd)

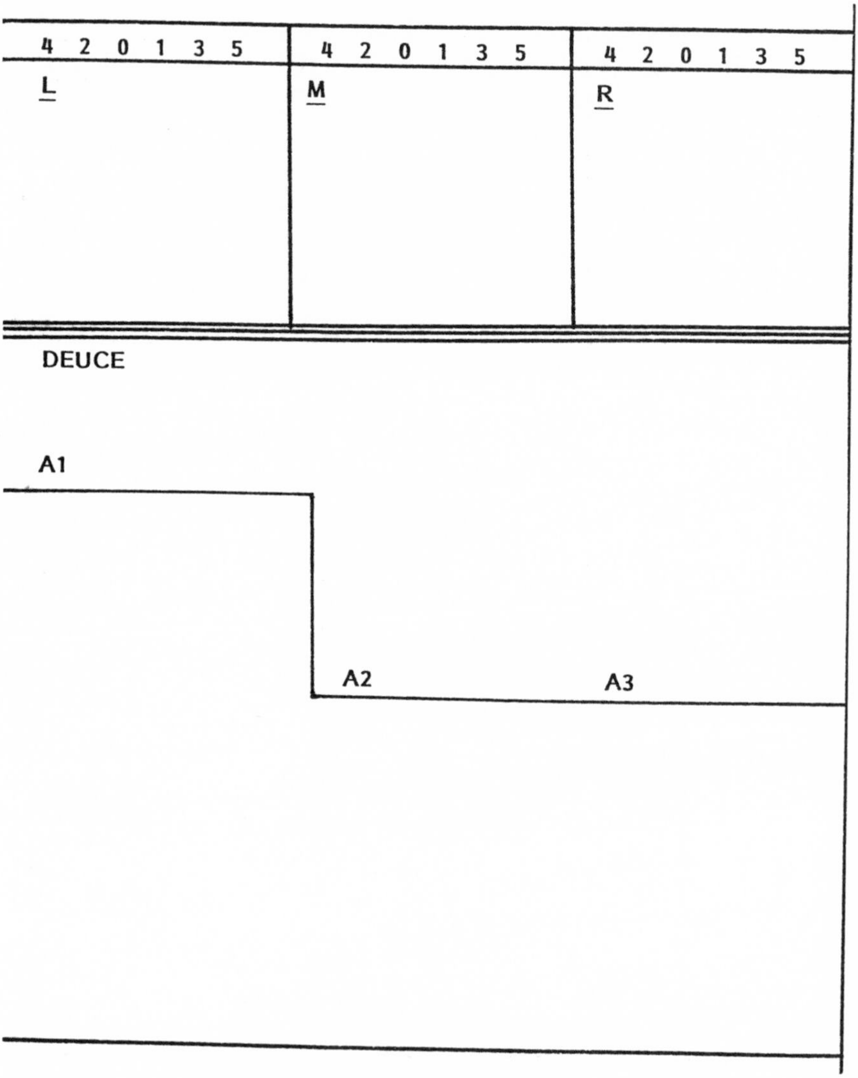

4 2 0 1 3 5	4 2 0 1 3 5	4 2 0 1 3 5
L	M	R

DEUCE

A1

A2   A3

DIAGRAM 9-3 (cont'd)

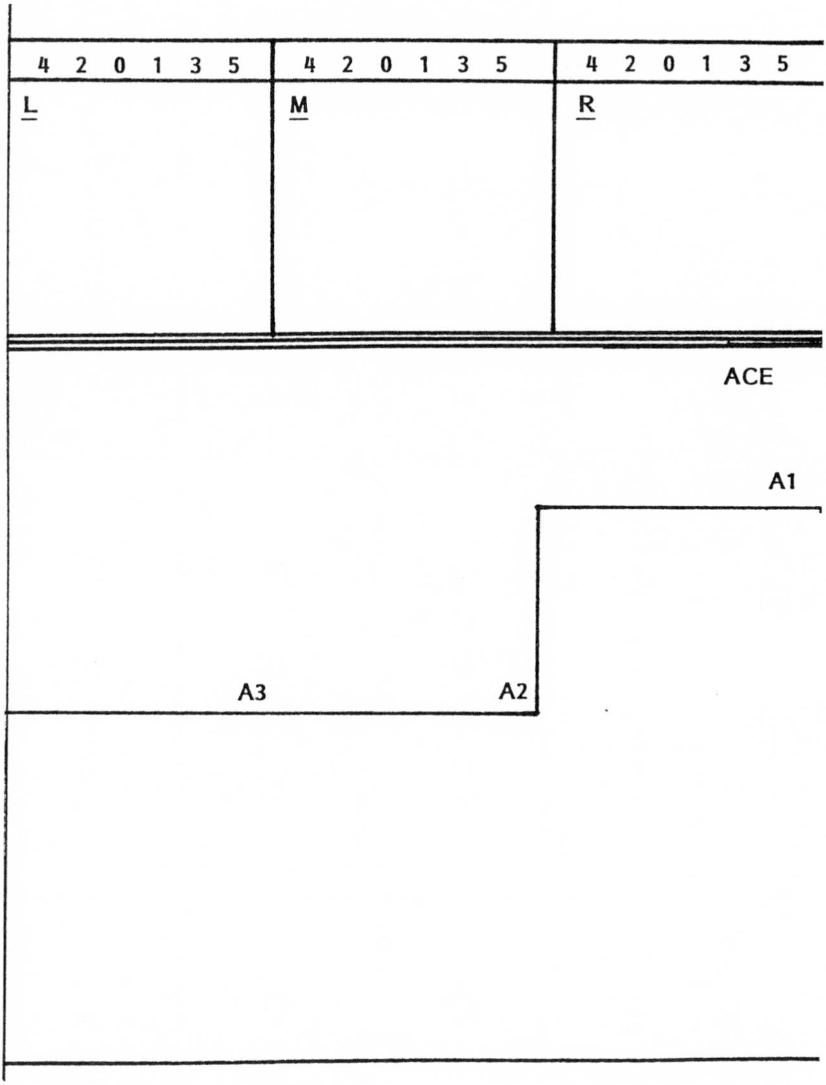

4	2	0	1	3	5		4	2	0	1	3	5		4	2	0	1	3	5
L							M							R					

ACE

A1

A3   A2

DIAGRAM 9-3 (cont'd)

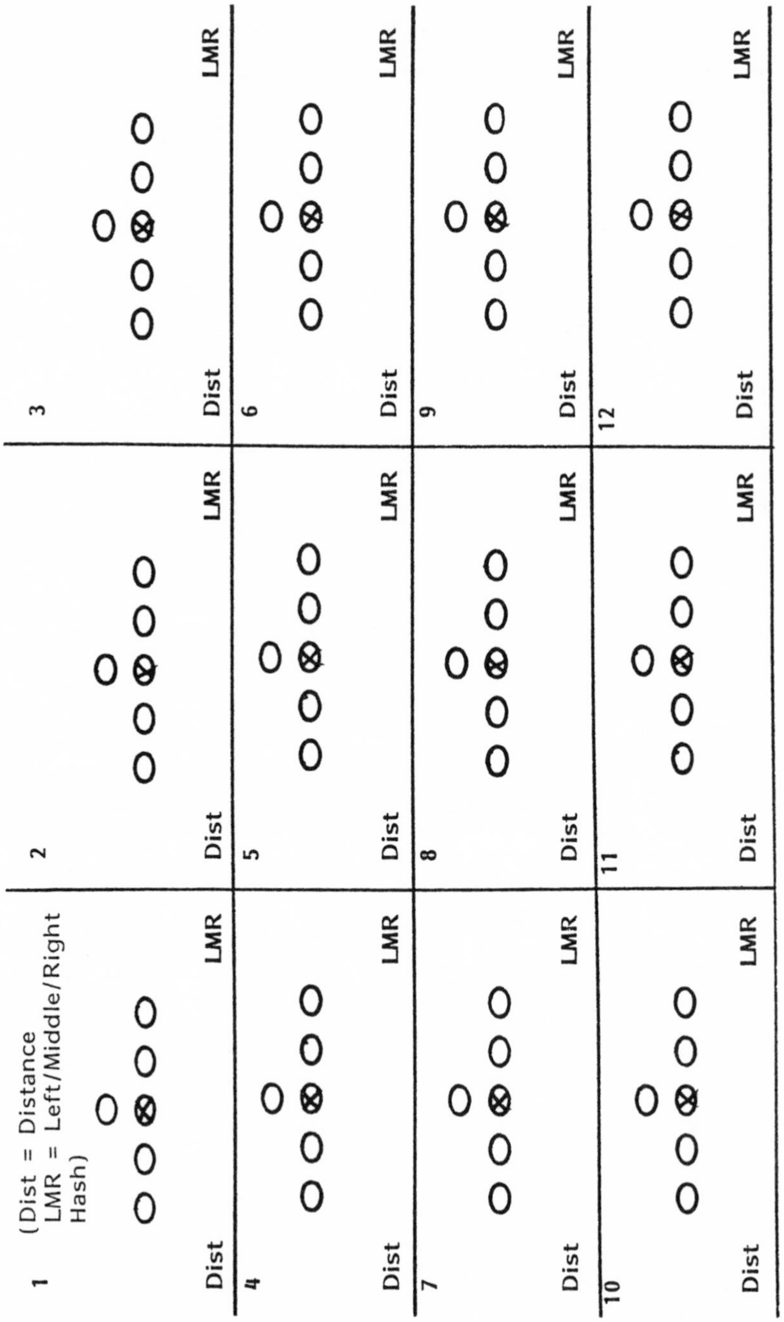

(Dist = Distance
LMR = Left/Middle/Right
Hash)

13 LMR Dist
14 LMR Dist
15 LMR Dist
16 LMR Dist
17 LMR Dist
18 LMR Dist
19 LMR Dist
20 LMR Dist
21 LMR Dist
22 LMR Dist
23 LMR Dist
24 LMR Dist
25 LMR Dist
26 LMR Dist
27 LMR Dist

DIAGRAM 9-3 (cont'd)

INCIDENTAL SETS

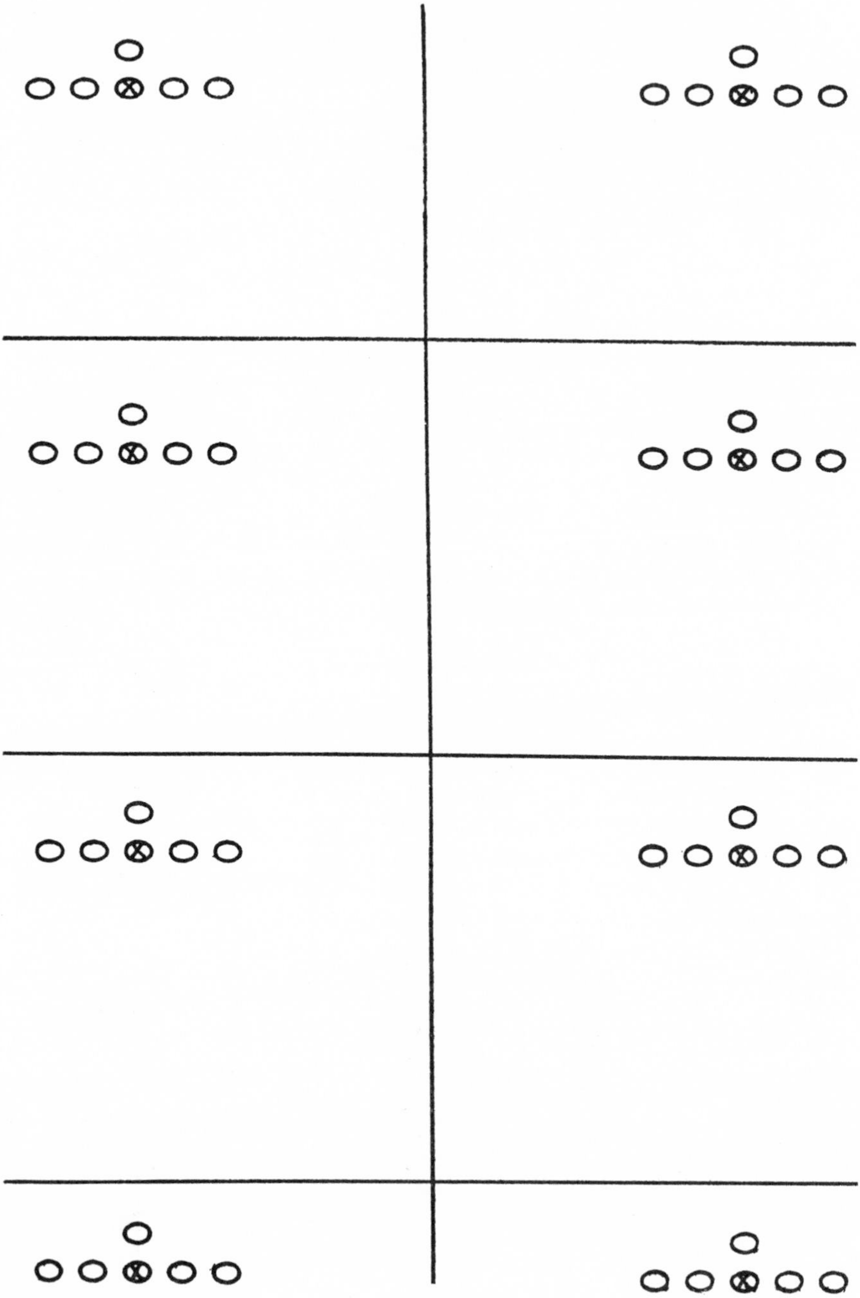

HARDING PRESS
P.O. BOX 141
HAWORTH, NJ 07641
(201) 767-7114

No. of Copies

HP001 DEFENSING THE DELAWARE WING-T
B. Kenig $12.00

_____

This coaching guide offers a successful answer to the
dynamic Wing-T. The innovative use of the 3-4
"Slant" and "Read Blitz" presents major problems for
this offense. All aspects of installing the "Slant" and
"Read Blitz" are detailed. The actual application of
these techniques is explained and diagrammed
against the basic Wing-T plays.

**HP002 FOOTBALL'S EXPLOSIVE MULTI-BONE
ATTACK**
T. DeMeo $12.00

_____

This innovative offense combines the explosiveness of
the Veer, the power of the I, the deception and misdirection of the Wing-T, the ball control of the
Wishbone and the wide-open play of the Pro Drop-
back Passing Attack. This book shows you how to tie
together the best of these offenses into one.

**HP003 COACHING RUN-AND-SHOOT
FOOTBALL**
A. Black $12.00

_____

Here is the first book on this exciting offense in more
than 20 years. This unique guide presents an attack
that can enhance your present offense or stand alone.
Coach Black gives you all the run-and-shoot pass
routes, plus blocking schemes, a complementary offense, a one-back running game, and much more.

Please send check, M.O., or school P.O. with your order.

Name _____   Subtotal: _____

Address _____   NJ Residents Only—

_____   7% Sales Tax: _____

City _____   *Shipping: _____

State _____ Zip _____   Total: _____

*Shipping: $2.00 first book; 75¢ each additional book